**Historical Atlases of South Asia,
Central Asia, and the Middle East ™**

A HISTORICAL ATLAS OF

INDIA

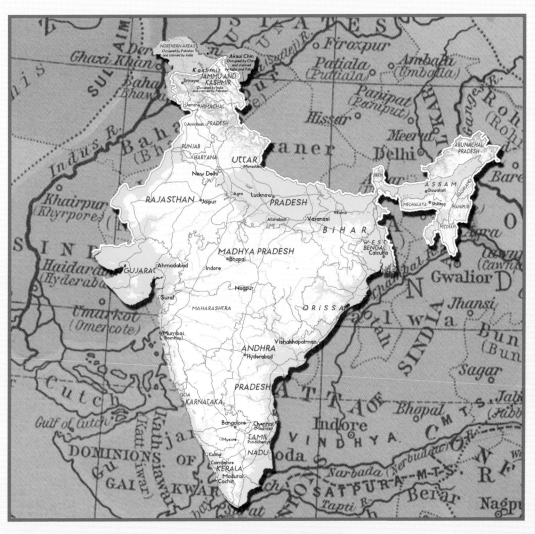

Aisha Khan

The Rosen Publishing Group, Inc., New York

To my brother Khalid, who would have been both amused and proud. I miss your intelligence, sharp critiques, acerbic humor, and trusting innocence.

Published in 2004 by The Rosen Publishing Group, Inc.
29 East 21st Street, New York, NY 10010

Copyright © 2004 by The Rosen Publishing Group, Inc.

First Edition

Library of Congress Cataloging-in-Publication Data

Khan, Aisha.
A historical atlas of India / Aisha Khan.
  p. cm. — (Historical atlases of South Asia, Central Asia, and the Middle East)
ISBN 0-8239-3977-4
1. India — History. I. Title. II. Series.
DS436.K46 2003
911'.54 — dc21

2003041405

Manufactured in the United States of America

Cover images (clockwise from top): The ancient Indian text of the Bhagavata Purana; a nineteenth-century Indian watercolor of Ranjit Singh, a leader of the Sikh kingdom of Punjab; and India's newly elected president, A. P. J. Abdul Kalam.

Contents

Introduction 5

1. The Harappan Civilization 8
2. Ancient Empires 13
3. Medieval Kingdoms 24
4. The Mughals 31
5. The British Raj 38
6. The Freedom Struggle 47
7. India After Independence 54

Timeline 60
Glossary 61
For More Information 62
For Further Reading 62
Bibliography 62
Index 63

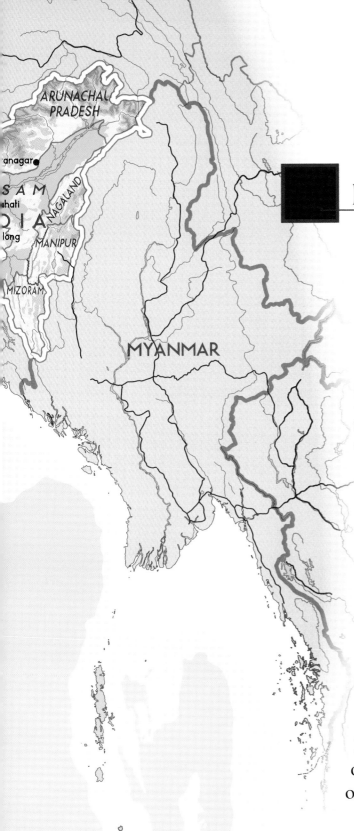

INTRODUCTION

India is a sizable country, the seventh-largest democracy in the world. Its territory, 1,222,559 square miles (3,166,414 square kilometers), encompasses an entire subcontinent. In the north, it consists of plains and valleys enclosed by the vast Himalaya Mountains, which stretch from east to west. In the south, India is a peninsula, jutting out into the Indian Ocean.

India has 5,892 miles (9,482 km) of land borders and 3,533 miles (5,686 km) of coastline. Its neighbors are Pakistan to the northwest; China, Nepal, and Bhutan to the north; Bangladesh, which is sandwiched by eastern Indian territory; and Myanmar to the northeast. Vast plains, lofty mountains, long rivers, and arid deserts comprise the Indian landscape. Possessing almost every type of climate, India is home to flora and fauna of all kinds.

India harbors some of the world's oldest settlements, some dating back 5,000 years. Since its earliest Indus valley civilizations, the region has been invaded by Arabs in the eighth century, Ottoman Turks in the twelfth century, and Europeans in the fifteenth century. British imperialism dominated India by the nineteenth century, until resistance to British colonialism under Jawaharlal Nehru, who became secular India's first prime minister in 1947, and Hindu pacifist Mohandas Gandhi helped make India independent from British rule. Although the modern government has made strides to improve the nation, the country still suffers from poverty, pollution, and overpopulation.

India, identified on this historical map of Asia as "Hindoostan," was, at the time of the map's design, in the grip of British colonial rule. And although Great Britain did provide the region with transportation systems, improved methods of education, and other modernization, after the departure of the British in 1947, 350 million Indians faced hunger, joblessness, poverty, and illiteracy. This map was first printed in 1808.

With more than 1 billion residents, India has the world's second-largest overall population. The majority of Indians are Hindus of varied divisions or sects, practices, and languages. Other religions include Islam, Sikhism, Christianity, Jainism, Buddhism, and Judaism.

The land that makes up the present nation of India has had a complex history. From ancient times, major portions of the territory have been settled, occupied, invaded, and developed. However, until present times, there were few occasions when the entire subcontinent was united under one government. Throughout most of India's history, its lands were split among a number of different kings and dynasties. Often, the southern peninsula had little to do with the northern regions. In fact, the language, culture, and customs of India's northern and southern regions vary significantly to this day.

When the British succeeded in conquering the subcontinent in the nineteenth century, they called it British India, and the name "India," derived from an ancient Greek name, Indica, stuck. In ancient Sanskrit, the land was referred to as Bharat or Bharatvarsh and, in medieval times, as Hindustan. These names are still used in India today.

Modern India is a country of contradictions. Although Indians are highly advanced in computer sciences, space, and nuclear technology, about 70 percent of the population currently lives in underdeveloped villages. The people in these rural communities survive as farmers, most without running water and electricity. Nearly half of India's population lives below the poverty line, making less than three dollars a day. As a result, India's government remains strained. Its greatest challenge is to provide a decent quality of life for all Indians while achieving the goal of an industrialized India.

1 THE HARAPPAN CIVILIZATION

Archaeologists have discovered evidence of human activity in India as far back as the Stone Age, from 400,000 to 200,000 BC. They have found stone tools and caves decorated with paintings.

In ancient times, human settlements usually emerged and thrived along rivers, in the adjacent fertile valleys. The remains of one of the world's oldest civilizations, dating back more than 4,000 years, were discovered in the nineteenth century in regions close to the Indus River. Now known as the Harappan Civilization, archaeologists have determined that it flourished between 3000 and 1500 BC.

The Discovery of Harappa

The Harappan Civilization is the first truly urban settlement in Indian history. Its remains were first discovered in the nineteenth century in

Mc

ARABIAN SEA

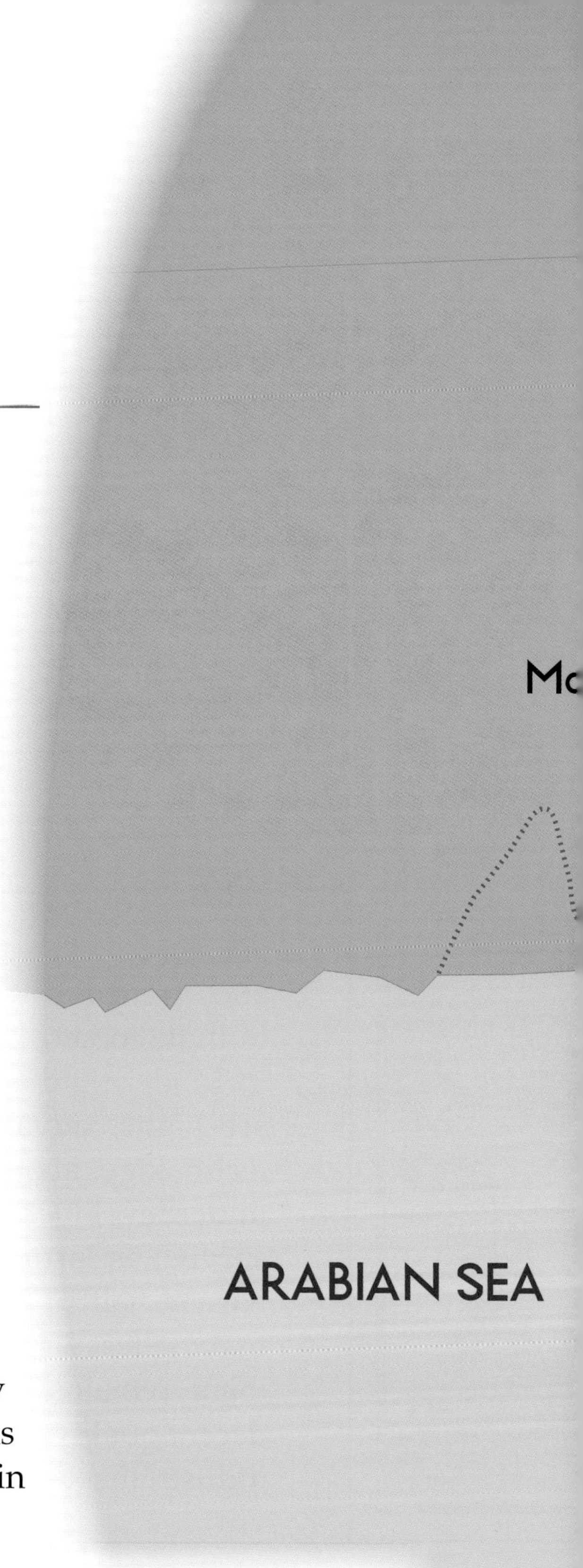

Archaeological discoveries in India have dated the region's history as far back as 5,000 years, as seen in this map showing Harappa, Mohenjo-Daro, and Kot Diji, all settlements in the Indus River valley. The indigenous people who populated India at this time were more sophisticated than previously believed. The ceramic carriage (bottom right), possibly a child's toy, was discovered in the ruins of Mohenjo-Daro and dates back to 2500 to 2000 BC. Other toys found on the site include balls, marbles, board games, and whistles.

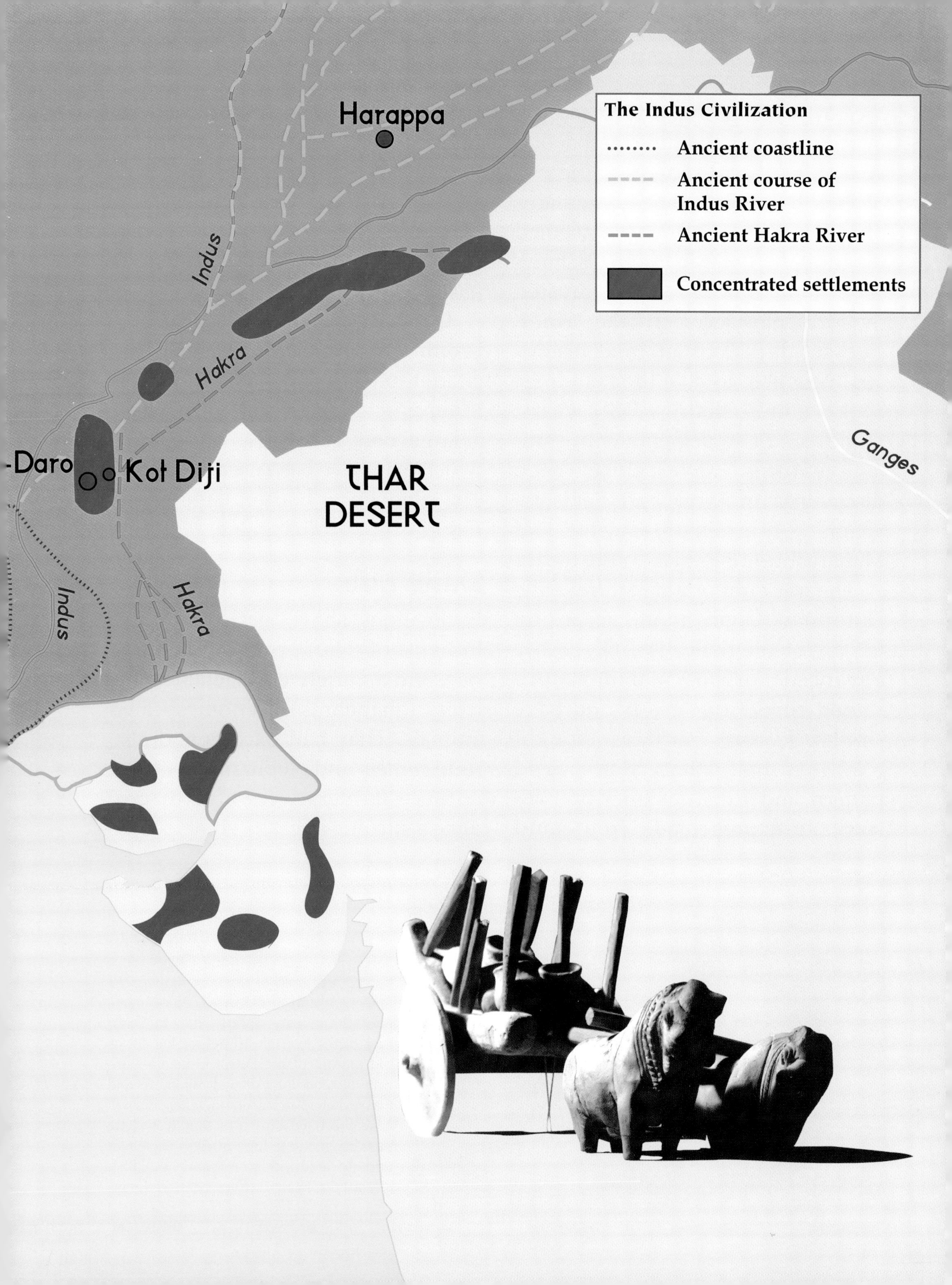

Harappa

The Indus Civilization
.... Ancient coastline
- - - Ancient course of
Indus River
- - - Ancient Hakra River
■ Concentrated settlements

Indus

Hakra

Ganges

-Daro ○ ○ Kol Diji

THAR
DESERT

Indus

Hakra

the town of Harappa, now located in Pakistan. At the time, archaeologists did not realize the significance of their discovery since the remains of the mud brick structures seemed too modern. Later in the 1920s, however, similar ruins were excavated in Mohenjo-Daro, in the Sindh (present-day Pakistan), and historians were able to date their findings back more than 4,000 years. Hundreds of settlements with similar features have since been discovered in India and Pakistan, spanning from Sindh, Gujarat, and Maharashtra to Punjab in the north.

The most important feature of the Harappan Civilization, according to archaeologists, is its highly advanced urban planning. All ruined cities from this period have similar features such as straight roadways that intersect in a grid pattern and identical one- or two-story structures made from mud brick. The larger structures had windows opening into inner courtyards, as well as private bathrooms and wells, and they were connected to a primitive underground sewage system. Other buildings seem to have been workshops for craftsmen.

Larger cities had a number of prominent buildings, including a citadel outside the main city. In Mohenjo-Daro, the citadel contained a large pool called the Great Bath, which may have been used for rituals. The citadel also housed large granaries to store surplus grains.

Daily Life

Excavations show that the ancient Indians of Harappa grew wheat, rice, and a variety of vegetables and fruits. Inhabitants kept domesticated animals. They had oxcarts and also rode camels and elephants.

Since farmers were able to produce a surplus of grain, some people

The archaeological site of Mohenjo-Daro, an Indus valley civilization located in present-day Pakistan, was first excavated in 1922. The Indus River once flowed just west of the city, making the area lush and fertile. Now, 5,000 years later, the Indus is about 1 mile (1.5 km) east of the site, an arid place known as the Mound of the Dead. Mohenjo-Daro was divided into distinct sections and was watched over from its tallest citadel, a semifortified structure that was quite possibly home to high priests. The Great Bath, located within one citadel building, might have been used for ritual bathing.

Harappan Seals

The seals found at various Harappan sites are considered among the most beautiful artistic objects of ancient India. Made of soapstone, the seals are small, flat, usually square, and marked with writing and human or animal motifs. Although historians have been unable to decipher the seals' markings, they may gain insight into daily life in ancient India. Some images indicate that ancient Indians may have worshiped a mother goddess; others show a man meditating in a yoga-like position. While the seals were likely used for sealing packages of goods for trade, historians believe they may have had some religious significance, too.

These small stone tablets, known as the Harappan seals, were most likely used as markers for the purposes of trading. It is widely believed that the people of the Indus valley traded with other nearby civilizations such as those located in Mesopotamia (Iraq).

became artisans. These Indians began making tools, weapons, household goods, and toys from copper and bronze. Cotton was woven and dyed for clothing. Pottery and bead-making were also common.

Factory-like structures for manufacturing tools, such as axes, chisels, arrowheads, knives, and seals, have been found near Mohenjo-Daro, indicating that some goods were mass-produced and traded throughout the Harappan territories. Artifacts like those found in Harappa have also been found in the Middle East and central Asia, showing that ancient Indians traded by sea and land with other civilizations. This view is reinforced by the discovery of a docking system at the port city of Lothal in western India. A system of uniform weights and measures was used, indicating the importance of trade. Seals have been found, marked with pictures and symbols, which historians believe were used to mark merchandise. The markings on the seals indicate that the ancient Indians had developed a script to

The gold button and bracelets seen in this photograph were discovered at the site of Mohenjo-Daro in Pakistan. Now housed at the National Museum of Pakistan in Karachi, they reveal much about the ancient artisans who created them, including the importing of precious metals into the city and the inhabitants' ability to create ornate designs and delicate beadwork. Other metal artifacts include bronze and silver bowls. The Indians who settled Mohenjo-Daro also wove their own cotton cloth and fastened their clothing with buttons.

record their language. Since the script has never been translated, it is still not known whether it is pictographic or alphabetic.

Decline of the Harappans

Archaeologists have noted that Harappan cities disappeared by 2000 BC. There are many theories for this decline. Some historians believe that Aryan invaders from central Asia attacked the Harappans and destroyed their civilization, replacing it with their own less-developed one. Others argue that the reasons for the decline were due to environmental changes. These changes could have included excessive flooding from the Indus River or possibly an epidemic that killed many and forced others to flee deeper into the Indian subcontinent. Historians have theorized that a likely combination of factors influenced this decline.

2 ANCIENT EMPIRES

After the decline of the Harappan Civilization, Aryans largely inhabited northern India. These pastoral nomads spoke an early form of Sanskrit known as Prakrit, which was later discovered to have similarities to ancient Greek and Latin. This led historians to conclude that the Aryans were originally inhabitants of eastern Europe and central Asia who spread in different directions.

The term "Aryan" means "noble or pure" and indicates the nomads' concern with maintaining a "pure" identity by keeping a distance from others. The Aryans over time collected a number of holy texts: the four Vedas, the Brahmanas, the Upanishads, and the Puranas. These texts, which were preserved orally until they were written down, provide an insight into the Aryans' belief systems and their way of life.

Through military superiority, Aryans established themselves as rulers over the existing inhabitants of north India and spread their social customs and religious beliefs. By 500 BC, Aryans had spread south to the Vindhya Range.

Daily Life

Initially nomadic herdsman, the Aryans later learned how to farm the land. They brought horses with

This text of the Bhagavata Purana is written in Sanskrit, the ancient literary language of India. Of the eighteen Puranas, the Bhagavata is the most popular, and its 18,000 verses have been translated into hundreds of languages and thousands of Indian dialects. Written in southern India during the eighth or ninth century, it is among the most important religious texts and celebrates the life of the Hindu god Krishna as the single supreme being. This manuscript is now housed in the National British Library in London, England.

They believed in a supreme being, called Brahman, but in daily worship, they prayed to Brahma, the creator; Vishnu, the sustainer; and Shiva, the destroyer, as well as a number of other gods.

The Aryans were a patriarchal, tribal people who placed a great deal of importance on birth and kinship. Clans formed a village, and several villages formed a tribe, headed by a *raja* (chief), who took advice from a council.

Society was divided on *varnas*, a concept that survives today as the caste system. It was originally based on three principles: *varna* (color), *ashrama* (stages of life), and *dharma* (duty). The Aryans, who were lighter in complexion than the natives, maintained this distinction by limiting contact between people of different varnas.

them and were skilled in riding horse-drawn chariots. They also used iron implements, including plows, which were pulled by oxen.

Cattle were very important to the Aryans, and the number of cattle a person owned indicated his or her wealth. To this end, it was common for tribal chiefs to lead attacks on neighboring tribes to steal cattle and thereby increase the tribe's wealth.

The Aryans followed an early form of Hinduism, worshiping many gods.

Indian Literature

The *Mahabharata* and the *Ramayana* are two important epic poems that illustrate Hindu beliefs. The *Mahabharata* is the story of a great battle between rival cousins, the Kurus and the Pandavas, over their grandfather's kingdom. The Pandavas did not want to fight their own blood cousins, but the gods explained to them that *dharma* (duty) comes before family and that they had to do what was right, not what they liked. This message was delivered by the god Krishna, an incarnation of Vishnu, who helped the Pandavas defeat the Kurus.

The *Ramayana* is about the victory of good over evil as shown through the adventures of Ram, a prince, who is thrown into exile by a scheming stepmother. While in exile, Ram rescues his wife, Sita, who is kidnapped by a powerful demon king, Ravan. In the end, Ram comes back to his kingdom as king, an event that is celebrated every year in the Indian festival of Diwali.

The beautiful mural pictured here, a detail depicting a story told in the Indian epic poem the *Ramayana*, was created in Bangkok, Thailand. It illustrates the moment when Ram's army crossed over a giant monkey who used his body to make a bridge in order for the army to rescue Ram's wife, Sita, who was held captive by evil King Ravan.

The Aryans had four varnas or castes that determined position in society as well as occupation: The highest was the Brahmin (priest), followed by Kshatriya (warrior), then Vaishya (merchant), and finally Shudra (servant class). Some people, considered too low to have a varna, were called *dasas* (servants) or *mlechhas* (untouchables) and had to live outside towns and villages.

Early States

The system of tribal chieftains evolved gradually into regional republics or hereditary monarchies. These new states built cities funded by taxes and had standing armies. A Buddhist text of the time mentions sixteen important states stretched across the Ganges-Yamuna and Indus River plains, including

Buddhism

Buddhism developed in the sixth century BC in northeast India from the teachings of Gautama Buddha. Buddha was originally a prince named Siddhartha, who was dissatisfied with his royal life and troubled by the sorrow, sickness, and greed he saw around him. He gave up his title and went into seclusion to meditate. Based on his observances, the Buddha stated that there were Four Noble Truths: the truth of misery (the human experience), the truth that misery is caused by desire, the truth that this desire can be ended, and the truth that this can be achieved by following a righteous path. From India, Buddhism spread to Southeast Asia, China, and Japan, where it is still practiced today.

The Indian Buddhists pictured in this photograph are sitting under a sacred bodhi tree, the same species of tree under which Gautama Buddha sought enlightenment through meditation thousands of years earlier.

This nineteenth-century Indian painting of the Hindu god Vishnu, illustrated here as the preserver of the universe and represented as the whole world, is decidedly Indian in style and was crafted in Jaipur. Other works of this period were highly influenced by European artists, a dramatic turn from traditional styles after the beginning of the British colonial period in India from about 1800. This painting is now part of the collection of works at the Victoria and Albert Museum in London, England.

Magadh and Anga in eastern India, Gandhara and Cambuja in the west, and Kasi and Koshala in the north. The period was marked by wars among the states for control of agricultural lands or trade routes, both important sources of taxes.

In 327 BC, Alexander the Great, a Greek emperor whose territories were known as the Macedonian Empire, also conquered territory in northwest India. His army, however, refused to move east of the Beas River in Punjab, so he turned back and died soon after. The lands he conquered were divided among his generals, with Seleucus controlling the Persian and Indian territories.

The Mauryan Empire

Around this time, Magadh gained dominance in northern India through its conquests of neighboring states under the ruler Bimbisara. By 322 BC, his descendant Chandragupta Maurya, who reigned between 324 and 301 BC, established the first Indian empire.

A Greek ambassador, Megasthenes, wrote his impressions of Magadh in the *Indica*. He described Magadh as a commercial center and its capital, Pataliputra (modern-day Patna), as a city of magnificent palaces, temples, learning centers, gardens, and parks. There was a highly structured and centralized government maintained by a large bureaucracy, which regulated taxes, trade, industries, mining, public places, and a standing army.

Ashoka

The most important Mauryan emperor was Ashoka, Chandragupta's grandson, who ruled from 268 to 231 BC. While expanding the empire through military conquests, Ashoka was shocked by an especially

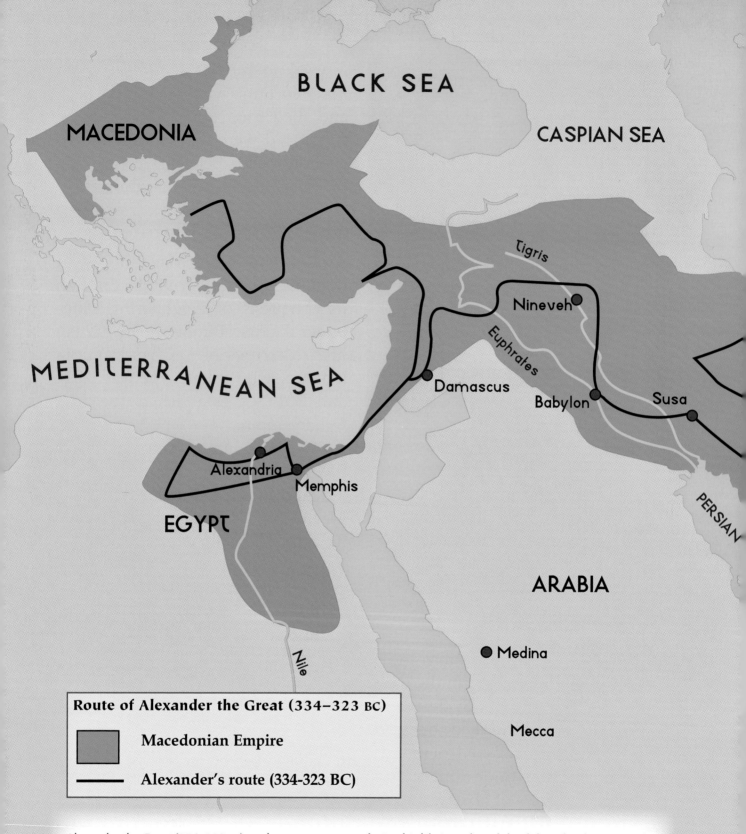

BLACK SEA

MACEDONIA

CASPIAN SEA

Tigris

Nineveh

MEDITERRANEAN SEA

Euphrates

Damascus

Babylon

Susa

PERSIAN

Alexandria

Memphis

EGYPT

ARABIA

Nile

● Medina

Mecca

Route of Alexander the Great (334–323 BC)

　　Macedonian Empire

　　Alexander's route (334-323 BC)

Alexander the Great (356–323 BC) made great conquests during his lifetime, though he did not live long enough to consolidate his territories. Seen as a dictator who wrongly assumed Persian costume and customs, Alexander had planned to extend his route farther into India's interior in 327 BC but was instead discouraged by his men, who wanted to return home after eight years of traveling. In the spring of 323 BC, he fell ill and died in the city of Babylon. The inset map shows how Alexander's territories were divided into kingdoms after his death. His followers, known as the Diadochi, included Antigonus I, Ptolemy I, Seleucus I, and Lysimachus.

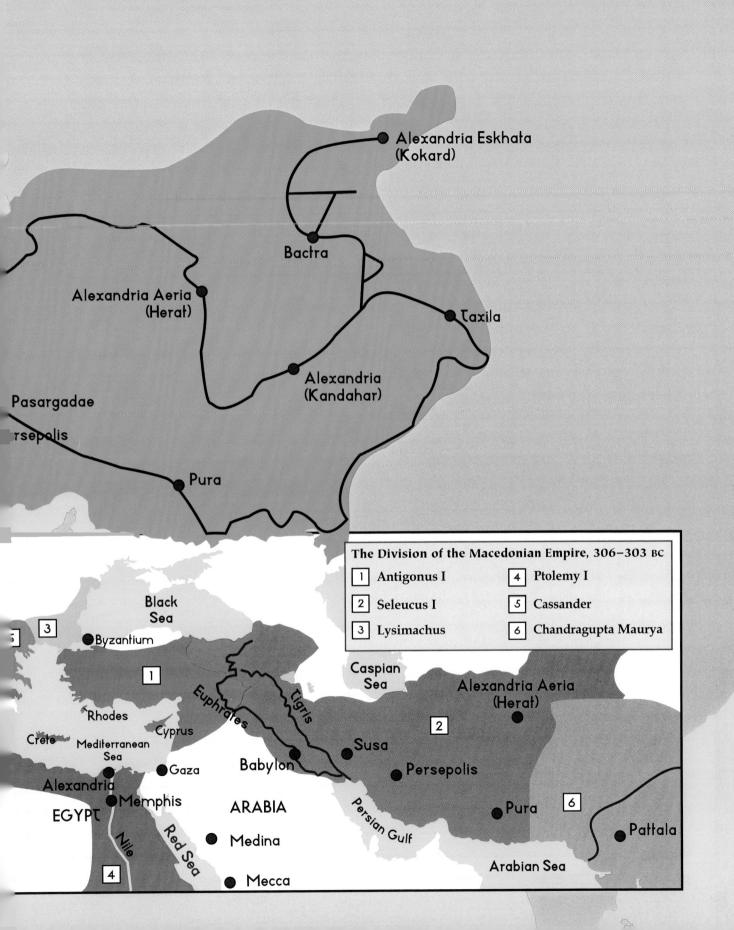

Alexandria Eskhata
(Kokard)

Bactra

Alexandria Aeria
(Herat)

Taxila

Alexandria
(Kandahar)

Pasargadae

rsepolis

Pura

The Division of the Macedonian Empire, 306–303 BC

1 Antigonus I   4 Ptolemy I

2 Seleucus I   5 Cassander

3 Lysimachus   6 Chandragupta Maurya

Black
Sea

3

Byzantium

1

Caspian
Sea

Alexandria Aeria
(Herat)

Euphrates

Tigris

2

Rhodes

Cyprus

Crete

Susa

Mediterranean
Sea

Babylon

Persepolis

Gaza

6

Alexandria

ARABIA

Pura

Memphis

Pattala

EGYPT

Nile

Red Sea

Medina

Persian Gulf

4

Arabian Sea

Mecca

bloody battle at Kalinga (Orissa), and he then adopted policies of *ahimsa* (nonviolence). In doing so, he converted to Buddhism and sent missionaries to central Asia, Sri Lanka, and Southeast Asia.

Ashoka issued edicts (laws) inscribed in Prakrit on stone pillars throughout his empire, which stretched from modern Afghanistan to Bangladesh, and to Karnataka in south India. Because of trade contacts with the Greeks and Romans, Ashoka also had edicts inscribed in Aramaic and Greek. Ashoka's successors were not as effective, and by 200 BC, the Mauryan Empire disintegrated. The Indian subcontinent was once again

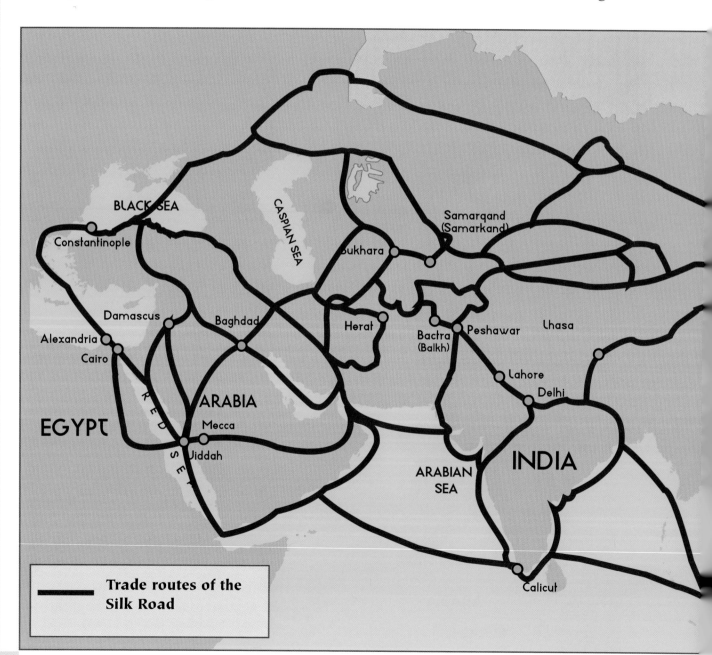

Trade routes of the
Silk Road

divided among a number of warring regional states.

The Kushanas

Like the Bactrians and Scythians before them, another nomadic people of central Asia, the Kushanas, invaded northwest India in 100 BC. The Kushanas controlled parts of Afghanistan, Iran, and northern India, from modern Peshawar in the west to Varanasi (Benares) in the east. They were an important link on the Silk Road, an ancient land and sea trade route that linked Asia with Arabia, Egypt, and parts of Europe. The Silk Road promoted trade among the Indians, Persians, Chinese, and Romans.

Under the Kushanas, the Gandharan school of art developed, marking a fusion of Greek and Indian styles as witnessed in beautiful sculptures of Buddha in stone, wood, and ivory.

The Guptas

After the Kushanas, the Gupta Empire arose across north India in AD 320. Because of the relative peace, development of classical Hinduism, and cultural achievements during this period, it is often described as India's Golden Age. The Guptas were, however, confined to the north, which was unified under the third king Chandragupta I and his successors, Samudragupta and Chandragupta II, who reigned together until 415.

The Gupta Empire marked great developments in religion, education, mathematics, art, and literature. The major principles of what would become modern Hinduism were established, including major gods, idol worship, and the importance of temples. A variety of subjects, including mathematics, medicine, and astronomy, also flourished. The Indian numeral and decimal systems, later spread by the Arabs and mistakenly called Arabic numerals, were invented during this period. Indians also developed herbal sciences and performed surgery, bone settings, and skin grafts.

The Gupta Empire was defeated in AD 500 by the Huns from central

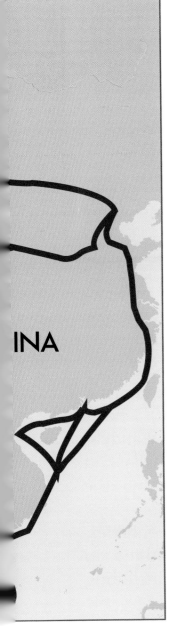

INA

The Silk Road—some 5,000 miles (8,047 km) of trade routes over land and sea—first emerged around 100 BC. Caravans traveling along these routes served merchants in foreign lands from Asia to the Mediterranean and introduced Westerners to exotic goods such as spices, ivory, jade, precious metals and gemstones, and Asian silks.

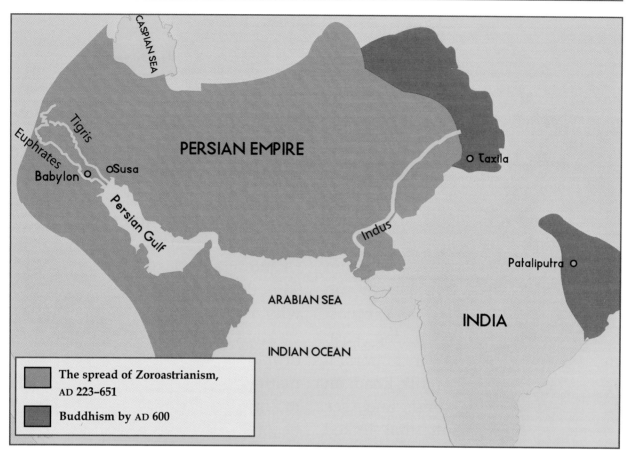

Though not as prevalent in India as Hinduism, other religions have had a following in the region, some as early as AD 223, as shown in this map. Long before Islam impacted India in the 700s, Zoroastrianism, proclaimed by the prophet Zoroaster, and Buddhism, proclaimed by Gautama Buddha, gained many converts. Both Buddhism and Zoroastrianism (its followers known as Parsees) are still practiced in modern India, as are Hinduism, Islam, Christianity, and Judaism.

Asia. A century later, the state of Kannauj gained prominence under Harsha Vardhan who became king in 606 and ruled for some forty years. Through military conquests, he briefly reunited north India.

The Deccan and the South

The Mauryans had incorporated parts of southern India into their empire. After their decline, a number of local kingdoms gained prominence, including the Satavahanas in the Deccan from 100 BC to AD 300, located in south-central India.

Below the Deccan, there were three prominent Tamil kingdoms—the Cheras (Malabar Coast), Cholas (Kaveri River valley), and Pandyas (Madurai, in Tamil Nadu)—that had never been conquered by the Mauryans.

Over the next few centuries, regional kingdoms continued to flourish in southern India, including the Chalukyas (556–757), the

This painting depicts Gautama Buddha and is a part of the remarkable frescoes that can be found inside the Ajanta caves, located in western central India. The caves, carved out of a steep ravine, were first discovered in 1819. They contain hundreds of exquisite examples of Buddhist art, including many scenes of Buddha's life, and were once a series of Buddhist monasteries dating from between 200 BC and AD 650.

Pallavas (300–888), and the Pandyas (500–1000). Many believe the inhabitants of southern India, called Dravidians, are the descendants of the Harappans. Over time, they adopted some aspects of northern Vedic culture, including Vedic Hinduism and the high status of Brahmins, but did not practice the varna system. Society was matriarchal, thus descent and identity were traced through mothers, not fathers.

Sustained by numerous rivers, the Dravidians had a highly developed agricultural system and had their own independent trade links with the world, including Rome, Arabia, and Southeast Asia. Madurai was a center of intellectual and literary activities.

The Hindu Dravidian rulers were tolerant and helped build Buddhist and Jain monuments, such as some of the famous cave temples of Ajanta and Ellora. By the mid-seventh century, Buddhism and Jainism began to decline, as Hindu cults of Shiva and Vishnu became more popular.

Although Sanskrit was the language of religion and learning in the south, too, the growth of religious cults strengthened the Dravidian languages: Tamil, Telugu, Malayalam, and Kannada.

3 MEDIEVAL KINGDOMS

The medieval period marked a series of changes in India. Larger kingdoms gave way to smaller, clan-based political units. Indian society, which was already divided on the basis of the caste system, was now also marked by feudalism. The feudal system was one where a class of landlords acted as intermediaries between the villagers and the rulers. The landlords controlled the lands and let peasant farmers live and work on the land, in return for a share of the crops. The landlords paid a portion to local nobles who in turn owed allegiance to regional kingdoms.

Feuding Lords

In the eighth century, most of northern India, up to the Deccan Plateau, was divided between three large dynasties. These kingdoms were the Palas in eastern India, the Pratiharas in western

This seventeenth-century map of Asia by Willem Janszoon Blaeu (1571–1638), a Dutch cartographer and printer, was first printed in a Dutch atlas in 1686. During his life, Blaeu was recognized as one of the world's best mapmakers, and his printing techniques, especially for duplicating maps, were also among the most respected. This original map is now located in the National Maritime Museum in Rotterdam, Holland.

Located on a hilltop in Jaipur, the Amber Fort is a massive complex of gateways and courts of Mughal splendor. Built over the course of two centuries beginning in 1592, the Amber Fort was built by Raja Man Singh, Mirza Raja Jai Singh, and Sawai Jai Singh. It is a fine example of Mughal and Rajput architecture, as is evident from its carvings, mirrors, and stucco work.

India and the northern plains, and the Rashtrakutas in the central plains and the Deccan.

These three kingdoms fought repeatedly for control of the fertile Upper Ganges valley, its city Kannauj, and the cross-country trade routes that ran through it. Historians have called this the Tripartite Struggle. For two centuries, each kingdom managed to seize Kannauj, but none could maintain a hold over it.

By the ninth century, the Palas and Pratiharas were in decline, and their feudal lords were trying to assert their independence from the king. The Rashtrakutas, pushing southward, moved their capital to the Deccan, but they also fell into decline by the end of the tenth century.

With the demise of the Palas, Pratiharas, and Rashtrakutas, northern and central India witnessed the rise of smaller states run by rulers who were lords under the former kings. These kings called themselves Rajputs, or "sons of kings," as they justified their rule by claiming to be of the Kshatriya warrior caste. Among these were the Chauhans, the later Pratiharas, the Solankis, the Chandellas, and the Parmars.

The Coming of Islam

In 711, a radically different culture was introduced to India. Arab armies entered the region around the Indus River and conquered modern-day Sindh. While Arabs had long sustained trade relations with India, they became further established with the conquest of Sindh, spreading their new religion, Islam, among the Indians. Arabs had also traded along the Malabar Coast in southern India for several centuries.

Islam, encouraged by the prophet Muhammad, developed in Arabia during the seventh century and soon spread throughout the Middle East. Islam is a monotheistic religion. Followers of Islam, called Muslims,

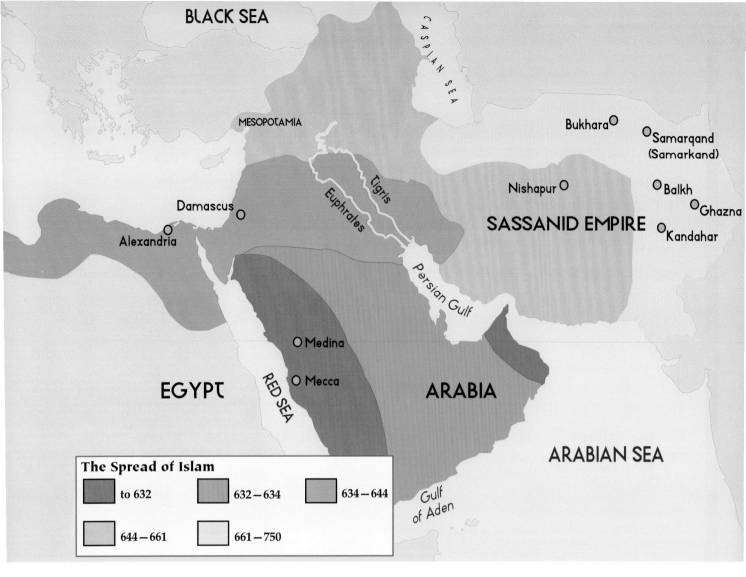

BLACK SEA

CASPIAN SEA

MESOPOTAMIA

Bukhara ○

○ Samarqand (Samarkand)

Nishapur ○

○ Balkh

○ Ghazna

SASSANID EMPIRE

○ Kandahar

Tigris

Euphrates

Damascus ○

Alexandria ○

Persian Gulf

○ Medina

○ Mecca

EGYPT

RED SEA

ARABIA

ARABIAN SEA

Gulf of Aden

The Spread of Islam

to 632

632 – 634

634 – 644

644 – 661

661 – 750

Although Islam is much different from Hinduism, the religion gained converts in India soon after the first arrival of invading Arab armies in AD 711. Many Indians welcomed Islam because of the equality it represented, freeing many Hindus from their lower castes. Within three decades, the religion of the Muslims had spread from Arabia to three continents: Asia, Africa, and Europe.

worship one god known to them as Allah. They believe that God has sent prophets—including Adam, Abraham, Moses, Jesus and Muhammad—to guide humans. Islam became popular among many Indians in medieval times because the religion teaches the equality of all humans. To the Hindu lower castes and untouchables, Islam gave them a chance to escape the caste system and rise in social status. Today, there are approximately 1.2 billion Muslims in the world, of which 130 million live in India, approximately 13 percent of the Indian population.

After Muhammad's death in 632, Muslims became divided into two sects, Shia and Sunni. The majority of Muslims are Sunnis and believe that Muhammad's successors should be chosen democratically, while the minority, called Shiites, argue that only blood descendants of Muhammad should rule the Muslim community.

While the Arabs did not move farther into India, Turkic tribes from Afghanistan and central Asia began a wave of conquests in the eleventh century that were to have a profound effect on Indian society for the next 600 years. The most notorious of these conquests were by the Afghan warlord Mahmud of Ghazni, who led seventeen raids between 997 and 1027 into north India, looting wealth from villages and conquering Punjab. Over the next century, these Turkic tribes, who were skilled horseback archers, continued to make inroads into north India.

The Delhi Sultanate

In the twelfth century, Muhammad of Ghor, a defeated Persian prince, made his way into northern India and conquered Punjab. He defeated the Rajput Chauhan king, Prithviraj, in the second battle of Tarain in 1192 (Ghor lost the first battle in 1191) and established his general, Qutubuddin Aibak, as governor of his Indian lands. Ghor died soon after, and Aibak established himself as sultan, or king. In doing so, he started the so-called Mamluk or slave dynasty because he was initially one of Ghor's slave soldiers.

Aibak's successors, including his granddaughter Raziya Sultan, likely India's first female ruler, were able to strengthen the sultanate. By 1290, the sultanate included the northern plains, Bengal, parts of the Deccan, and Rajasthan. After the Mamluks, there were a series of dynasties, including the Khaljis (1290–1320), the Tughlaqs (1320–1413), the

This is a present-day photograph of the mausoleum of Mahmud of Ghazni (971–1030), founder of the Ghaznavid dynasty. It is located in Ghazni, Afghanistan. Mahmud's conquests on the Indian subcontinent destroyed many Hindu temples, and he looted much Indian art and treasure. With this stolen wealth, the Ghaznavid dynasty established an Islamic center of culture in present-day Afghanistan and ruled for more than 200 years. Mahmud's successors ruled over a reduced domain from the capital at Lahore until 1186.

Sayyids (1414–1451), and the Lodis (1451–1526).

Each dynasty was involved in a constant restructuring of government and territory. Efforts by each dynasty to remain in power were made more difficult because each owed allegiance to competing factions in the royal court at Delhi. Ambitious noblemen would gather support of local feudal lords, such as the Hindu Rajput chiefs, to gain power and ultimately overthrow the sultan.

Turkic culture influenced Indian society, most notably with Islam. While the sultans theoretically ruled according to Islamic law, they actually compromised with Indians, creating situations to strengthen their government and increase their acceptance. While government positions were initially held only by Turkic Muslims, both Indian-born Muslims and Hindu chieftains eventually rose to positions of power in the sultanate.

Other Turkic influences included new methods of agriculture: canal irrigation and the Persian wheel. However, farmers were largely forced to turn over their harvest because of intermediaries who demanded a share of the produce. One sultan, Muhammad Tughlaq, even had to extend loans to the impoverished farmers, most of whom were later forgiven by his successor, Firuz.

Trade continued to flourish, and artisans further developed their wares, fueled, in part, by a demand of exotic goods by the nobility. These items included blown glass, silks, and stone carvings. Other Turkic influences came in the form of the spinning wheel and advancements in silk production.

South India

By the eighth century, the southern peninsula was divided among a number of stable kingdoms, including the Chalukyas and Cholas. The Cholas, with their capital at Thanjavur, were the dominant power in the southernmost regions, based on revenues generated from trade with east Africa, the Middle East, and Southeast Asia. Under the kings Rajaraja I and Rajendra, the kingdom spread north up to Andhra, west to the Malabar Coast, and north to Sri Lanka. The Cholas even launched a naval expedition against the Srivijaya kingdom in Java (Southeast Asia) to maintain their control over sea trade routes.

Large parts of the south were unaffected by the advent of the Persian-Turkic nobility in the north. The Delhi sultans tried repeatedly to spread south, but were stopped in the Deccan.

The Cholas had declined by the thirteenth century, and several new dynasties emerged, including the one started by Hasan Gangu in 1347. A Deccan governor under the Tughlaqs, he revolted and started the Bahmani sultanate. In 1527, the sultanate divided into five smaller kingdoms: Ahmadnagar, Berar, Bidar, Bijapur, and Golconda. The Bahmanis, who were Turks from the north, infused southern culture with their own. This combination led to a distinct "Deccani" style of food, clothing, architecture, and painting. Another important southern kingdom was the Vijayanagar Empire. Established by Harihara I in 1336 in what is now Karnataka, it soon covered most of the peninsula, from India's west coast to Madurai in the east.

The Bahmanis and Vijaynagars warred constantly in their attempts to control India's plains between the Krishna and Tungabhadra Rivers. In 1565, the rulers of the five kingdoms of what was once the Bahmani sultanate combined their forces and attacked Vijayanagar. This conflict was known as the Battle of Talikot.

4 THE MUGHALS

Mongols, a nomadic people, had already made several invasions into India. The pastoral Mongols were not unified until the early thirteenth century under Genghis Khan. By 1206, Genghis Khan had established a capital in Carakorum and reorganized his empire and armies in an attempt to gain territory and power. The strength of the Delhi sultanate was its ability to attack, loot, and always retreat. Timur (also called Tamerlane), a Mongol Turk, led one such devastating raid in 1398, looting Delhi and massacring many inhabitants. A descendant of Timur, Zahiruddin Babur, who was related to Genghis Khan, eventually established Mongol Turkish rule in India.

Babur

Babur, who reigned between 1526 and 1530, was forced to leave Samarkand (present-day Uzbekistan) by rivals and managed to conquer the region around modern Kabul, Afghanistan, in 1504. He continued into Punjab, where he combined forces with an Afghan chief to attack the Delhi sultanate. In 1526, Babur, believed to be leading an army of only 12,000 compared to Ibrahim Lodi's 100,000, defeated Lodi at the Battle of Panipat, about 56 miles (90 km) north of present-day Delhi. A year later, Babur put down an

The *Baburnama*, from which this image was taken, tells the history of Zahiruddin Babur (1483–1530), the first Mughal emperor. It depicts Babur in one of his many gardens, this one in Kabul, Afghanistan. When the emperor entered India with his armies in 1526, it was the first time that firearms were used on the subcontinent.

By the time of Babur's death in 1530, many of the rulers he had defeated asserted their independence, forcing Babur's son, Humayun, to flee to Persia in 1543. From there, Humayun slowly conquered his way through Afghanistan in 1545. Finally, twelve years after going into exile, Humayun took back Delhi in 1555, defeating the powerful Afghan sultan, Sher Shah Suri. He was unable to enjoy his victory, however, dying a year later in 1556. His throne was left to his teenage son, Jalaluddin Akbar.

uprising led by a group of Rajput chiefs. In 1529, he conquered Bengal but died in 1530 before he could consolidate his territories.

Babur kept a journal, which has survived as the *Baburnama*. He was renowned as a nature lover and had several gardens built in Kabul, Lahore, and Agra. He also kept detailed accounts of the flora and fauna he encountered in his memoirs.

Akbar

Akbar is regarded as not only the greatest of the Mughal emperors but also one of the greatest Indian rulers of all time. Initially, because of his age, he ruled under the advice of a regent, his father's general, Bairam Khan. By 1560, Akbar took over. Now seventeen years old and illiterate (historians believe he was dyslexic), he nonetheless loved to learn. He had books read

This image is from the *Akbarnama*, Akbar's biography written by the emperor's confidant, Abul Fazl. Akbar (1543–1605) was a furious warlord who intensified loyal Indian armies but was spiritually open-minded, granting many positions of power to Hindus and later organizing a religion based upon his own beliefs. This image depicts one of Akbar's many expeditions.

to him constantly and invited scholars of all disciplines to his court to discuss art, science, philosophy, and religion.

When Akbar inherited the throne, his territories comprised only Delhi and Punjab. But through a series of successful wars, his empire soon stretched from present-day Kabul, Afghanistan, throughout most of central India. Akbar moved his capital from Delhi to Agra in 1571, building a magnificent walled city known as Fatehpur Sikri. Later his capital moved again, to Lahore in 1585 and back to Agra in 1599.

Akbar implemented policies to strengthen his grip over his vast holdings. He divided it into fifteen provinces and established loyal *zamindars*, or landlords, who collected revenue for him and kept a portion as payment. Above the landlords were local nobles called *mansabdars*, who maintained troops loyal to the emperor. With his Hindu adviser, Todar Mal, he devised a tax system that provided maximum benefit to the state but was bearable for the farmers. He also improved communications by developing highways linking the distant corners of his empire. In this he was helped by his father's enemy, Sher Shah Suri, who had already built the Grand Trunk Road, linking Patna to Kabul. The road network increased trade, as

Internationally renowned for its beauty and splendor, the Taj Mahal, located in India's city of Agra, in the state of Uttar Pradesh, is undoubtedly the world's greatest mausoleum. Built during the reign of Mughal emperor Shah Jahan in honor of his wife, Arjumand Banu, who later became known as Mumtaz Mahal, the seventeenth-century structure has held her remains since 1630, when she died during childbirth. The emperor joined her after his death in 1666.

goods could now move easily from villages to distant cities and ports.

Akbar also incorporated more Hindus into his government and married princesses from Rajput families. He funded temples, participated in Hindu festivals, and abolished the *jizya* (poll tax) imposed on non-Muslims. He even invented his own religion, Din-i-Ilahi (Divine Faith), which consisted of principles from all faiths. He tried to reform Hinduism, which did not allow widows to remarry and forced them to commit suicide when their husbands died.

After ruling for forty-nine years, Akbar was succeeded by his son, Jahangir, who reigned from 1605 to 1627. The reign of Akbar's grandson Shah Jahan followed, from 1628 to 1658. Jahangir and Shah Jahan maintained the prosperity of the empire and devoted their rule to building magnificent gardens and monuments and promoting the arts, including poetry, music, dance, and painting, leading to a new fusion of Persian and Indian styles. Shah Jahan was especially fond of architecture, building the Jama Masjid (Friday Mosque) and the Red Fort in Delhi, and the exquisite Taj Mahal in Agra.

At the same time, the distant borders of the empire, especially in the northwest and the south, were subject to invasions. Shah Jahan was forced to send Mughal armies to reconquer the Deccan and Kabul. Over time, local governors tried to shake off Mughal control and create independent states. Shah Jahan's son and successor, Aurangzeb, later faced these consequences.

The Beginning of the End

Aurangzeb gained the throne in 1658 much like his father and grandfather had, by killing all his rivals. At one point, he even imprisoned his own father. Aurangzeb launched successful military campaigns, extending the empire to its greatest limits, including Mysore and Madras in the south,

Sikhism

The Sikh religion arose in the fifteenth century in Punjab under the teachings of Guru Nanak. Nanak was dismayed by religious differences. He preached a new creed that was a combination of folk Hinduism and mystical Islam, and it soon became popular among farmers. Sikhs became involved in Mughal politics, when the fourth successor of Nanak, Guru Arjun, supported Khusrau, Jahangir's son, in his attempt to overthrow Jahangir. When the bid failed, Jahangir reportedly had Arjun killed. That event caused immense hatred for Mughal rule among the Sikhs, for which was increased by Aurangzeb's repressive leadership.

This nineteenth-century Indian watercolor depicts the bodyguards of Ranjit Singh (1780–1839), a leader of the Sikh kingdom of Punjab, on horseback with matchlock rifles. The founder of the Sikh religion, Guru Nanak (1469–1539), experienced a religious epiphany at thirty years of age that enlightened him to begin a new faith.

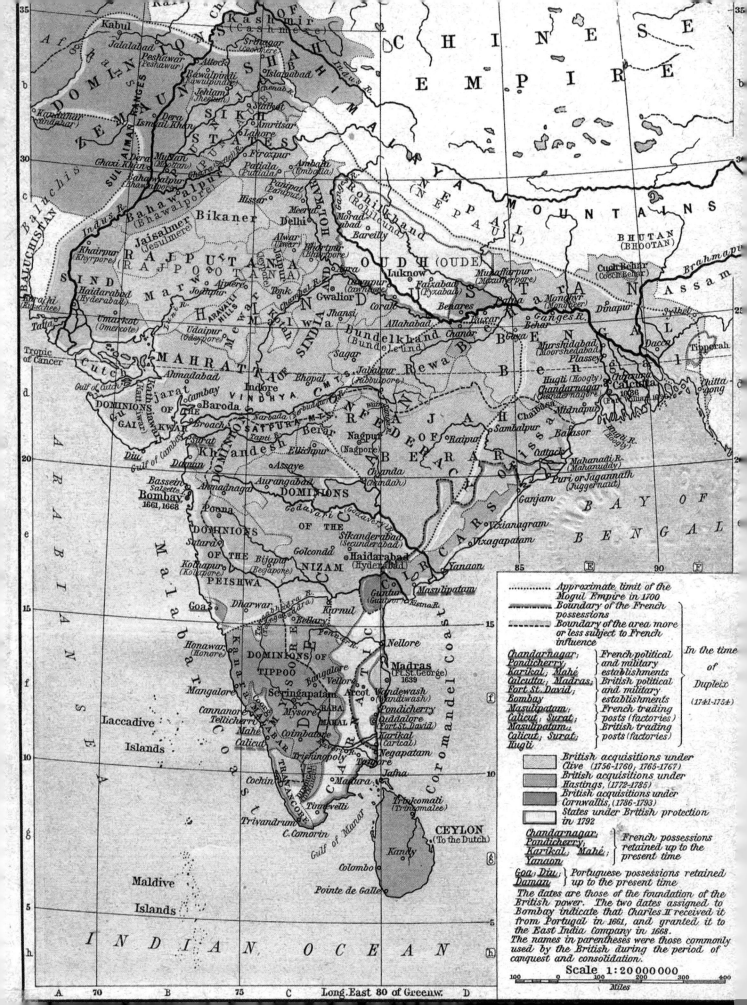

and parts of Burma (Myanmar) in the east. However, the empire was too large to control effectively, and he had to rely on governors and former kings for assistance. His army had also lost its edge, failing to keep up with new military technology.

Soon there were numerous uprisings throughout the empire. And Aurangzeb, despite his efforts, was unable to prevent the decline. A stern man and strict Muslim, he was unable to generate loyalty and support among his nobles, largely because of his personality. He alienated the Hindu population by his severe implementation of Islamic law, especially the reimposition of taxes on non-Muslims. Most of his rule was spent in different parts of the empire, trying to put down the chaos of revolt. From Afghanistan to Bengal to the Deccan, he was constantly on the road and engaged in battle.

It was at this time that two significant regional powers arose, the Marathas and the Sikhs. The Marathas were peasant warriors of western India, and under Shivaji Bhonsle (1627–1680), they rose in rebellion against the Mughal Empire. The Sikhs in Punjab also posed a problem, as they attempted to free themselves from Mughal rule. Neither succeeded under Aurangzeb's fifty-year reign, but it was clear that the days of the great Mughal Empire were numbered.

Aurangzeb died in 1707 and was followed by weak successors. Delhi was looted twice, once by the Persian Nadir Shah and later by the Afghan Ahmad Shah Abdali. By this time, the Marathas and Sikhs, as well as another peasant group, the Jats of north India, were semi-independent. Governors also only paid nominal allegiance to the emperor. However, the final deadly blow to Mughal might was dealt by another, stronger force that emerged on the subcontinent: the Europeans.

This historical map of India (left) illustrates how the subcontinent was radically changed during the early colonial period from 1700 to 1792. First printed in William R. Shepherd's *Historical Atlas* in 1923, it identifies British, French, and Portuguese military and trading posts and the annexed lands of India under several British generals, including Robert Clive (1725–1774), Warren Hastings (1732–1818), and Charles Cornwallis (1738–1805).

5 THE BRITISH RAJ

From ancient times, India had traded exotic spices, textiles, sugar, and handicrafts with the West. In an effort to gain less expensive access to Indian goods, Europeans began searching for direct sea routes to India. Finally, in 1498, the Portuguese navigator Vasco da Gama landed in Calicut (Kerala), marking a new era of European intervention in Indian affairs.

Over the next two centuries, European traders, including the Dutch, English, Portuguese, and French, also traveled to India to buy goods. To do so, they established trading posts along India's coast. As the Mughal Empire weakened, however, Europeans began to play politics. Their trading outposts eventually resembled fortresses. They maintained larger armies, and their ambitions grew.

This map of southern India was created around the time of the British annexation of many of the country's princely states. Although the British claimed that they were helping to civilize India with laws and a reliable system of justice, their trading rules and practices quickly became corrupt. Eventually an Indian movement to create a stronger sense of nationalism grew, beginning in part with the Indian Rebellion of 1857–1858, and with the leadership of Mahatma Gandhi and Jawaharlal Nehru.

The British East India Company

The British arrived in India in the form of the East India Trading Company, which had a monopoly from Queen Elizabeth I to import goods from India. It set up bases in Surat (Gujarat), Hughli (Bengal), Madras, and later Bombay (Mumbai).

The company concentrated on trade initially, especially after it lost a battle against Aurangzeb. After his death, the British became bolder. Eventually they persuaded a successor, Farrukhsiyar, to give them a *firman* (grant) in 1717 allowing the company trading concessions and the right to collect revenue from some villages near Calcutta.

The British began interfering in local politics, loaning their army to warring princes. Led by Robert Clive, the company fought several successful wars with the French for control of Arcot (near Madras) from 1744 to 1763.

The company's first major success came in Bengal, where it defeated the Mughal governor Sirajuddaula, in the Battle of Plassey in 1757. The Mughals took on the company in the Battle of Buxar in 1765, but lost again. Emperor Shah Alam was forced to grant the company the province of Bengal, including rights to govern and collect taxes from its inhabitants. Shortly thereafter, Clive became the first British governor of Bengal.

Territorial Conquests

With the conquest of Bengal, the company became a

In this eighteenth-century British portrait by Edward Penny, the celebrated British general Robert Clive is pictured receiving a grant of money from the Nawab of Bengal. Many Britons became wealthy after working in India during the colonial period.

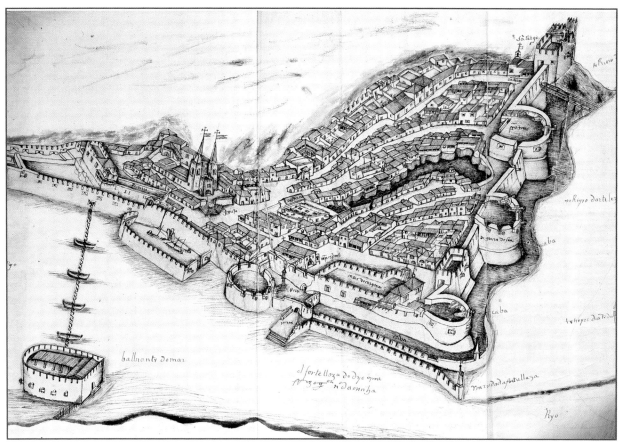

The historical map depicts a Portuguese trading post and colony in Diu, in western India, during the sixteenth century. The Portuguese were less successful than the British colonists because they immediately attempted to introduce Christianity in India and often plundered Arab vessels.

regional government. It now had access to huge sums of money and the means to bribe local traders to sell Indian goods to it at cheaper rates. Its greed caused a famine in Bengal in 1771, killing 5 million people who were too poor to buy food. All their money had gone to the British.

Although the company was privately run, concern by the Indian government led to the passing of the Regulating Act (1773) and Pitt's India Act (1784). The company was now answerable to Parliament through a board of control headed by a governor-general based in Calcutta.

At the same time, the company continued to annex India's land. Using flimsy excuses, it attacked any prince it thought was hindering profits. The company fought wars against the Marathas, Rajputs, Tipu Sultan of Mysore, and the Sikhs, ultimately bringing them under its control. Sometimes it let the prince remain, but only as its puppet leader. The company called this the "subsidiary alliance." The prince got to keep his

British Nabobs

Nawab means "prince" or "governor." The British officials of the East India Company made so much money in the form of illegal bribes, kickbacks, and commissions, as well as private trade and investments, that when they returned to England they led lavish lifestyles. People started calling them "nabobs." Soon it became common for upper-class British families that were financially strapped to send their sons to India to "make their fortunes."

throne, as long as he accepted the company's authority, paid its army, and paid other annual taxes.

A later governor-general, Lord Dalhousie, added the "doctrine of lapse" to the subsidiary alliance. He decided that if a prince died without a son, he could not adopt an heir; the British would take over his state. Dalhousie used this to annex many states throughout India.

Economic Consequences

During this time, the nature of trade also changed, with grave consequences for India. When they first came, the British bought finished goods such as woven cloth, processed sugar, spices, and handicrafts. But they had to pay for them in either gold or silver. To avoid this, they started offering goods they got from other countries, such as China, as payment. As industry developed in Britain, officials bought raw goods instead of finished ones, such as raw cotton instead of finished cloth for the textile mills in Britain. On top of that, Britain would ship its factory-made cloth to India, making sure it was available to purchase at less expensive rates by imposing heavy taxes on Indian-made cloth. Soon Indian craftsmen lost their livelihood, becoming day laborers. The British then took their profits, along with India's minerals, like iron and coal, for use in Britain. Even the railways and telegraph they had developed were paid for by Indian taxes and helped them exploit India more efficiently.

It is in these ways that Britain became an imperial power. Imperialism is when a nation conquers other countries and controls their economies, using those countries' environmental and human resources

This historical map of India in 1760 during the time of British general Robert Clive was first printed in 1905. Clive spent his life advancing in the British military, with his most famous and important conflict fought in 1757, the Battle of Plassey, a victory that furthered the British domination of India. Clive truly believed in the British imperialistic ideas behind his mission, and he felt that to exploit India's resources and wealth was beneficial for Britain and the entire world.

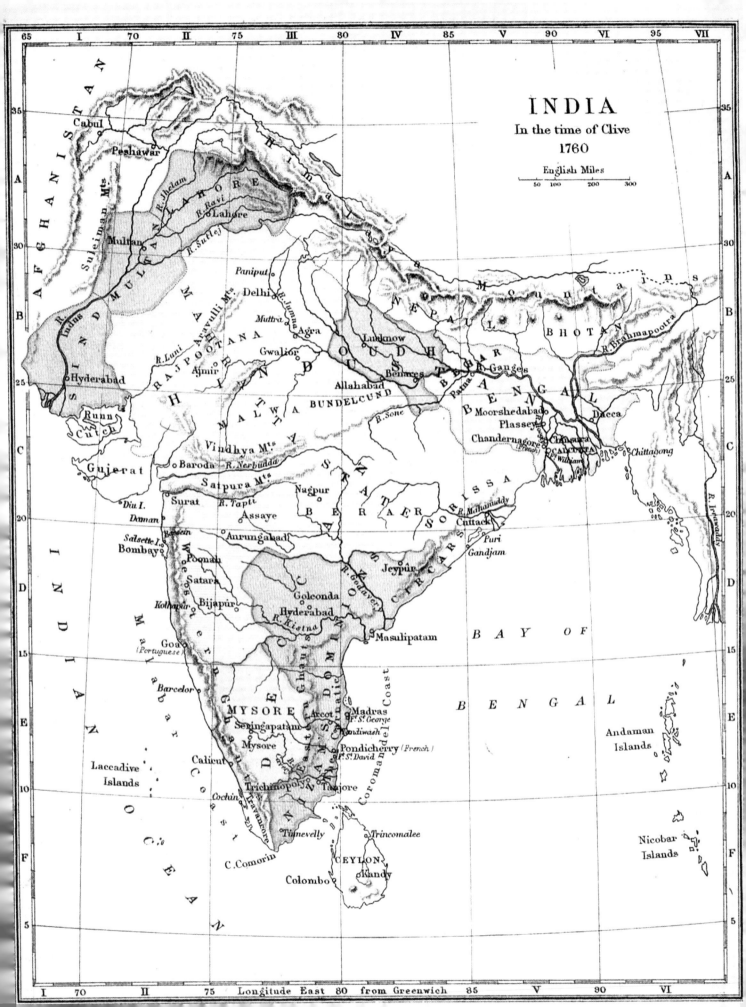

| 65 | I | 70 | II | 75 | III | 80 | IV | 85 | V | 90 | VI | 95 | VII |

INDIA
In the time of Clive
1760

English Miles

50   100   200   300

AFGHANISTAN

Cabul

Peshawar

Suleiman Mts.

R. Jhelum

LAHORE

R. Ravi

Lahore

R. Sutlej

Multan

MULTAN

Himalaya Mountains

NEPAUL

BHOTAN

R. Brahmapootra

R. Indus

SINDH

Hyderabad

Runn of Cutch

Gujerat

RAJPOOTANA

Aravulli Mts.

R. Luni

Ajmir

Paniput

Delhi

R. Jumna

Muttra

Agra

Gwalior

Lucknow

OUDH

Benares

Allahabad

HINDOSTAN

MALWA

BUNDELCUND

R. Sone

Patna

BEHAR

BENGAL

Moorshedabad

Plassey

Dacca

Chandernagore (French)

Chinsura

CALCUTTA

Ft. William

Chittagong

Diu I.

Daman

Baroda

R. Nerbudda

Vindhya Mts.

Satpura Mts.

Surat

R. Tapti

Nagpur

Assaye

BERAR

GREATER MAHRATTA

ORISSA

R. Mahanuddy

Cuttack

Puri

Gandjam

Salsette I.

Bombay

Bassein

Poonah

Satara

Kolhapur

Bijapur

Western Ghauts

Golconda

Hyderabad

R. Kistna

R. Godavery

NIZAM'S DOMINION

NORTHERN CIRCARS

Jeypûr

Masulipatam

BAY OF BENGAL

Goa (Portuguese)

Barcelor

Malabar Coast

MYSORE

Seringapatam

Mysore

Calicut

Arcot

Conjeveram

Madras

Ft. St. George

Wandiwash

Pondicherry (French)

Ft. St. David

Eastern Ghauts

CARNATIC

Coromandel Coast

TANJORE

Trichinopoly

Tanjore

Travancore

Cochin

Tinnevelly

C. Comorin

Trincomalee

CEYLON

Colombo

Kandy

INDIAN OCEAN

Laccadive Islands

Andaman Islands

Nicobar Islands

R. Irrawaddy

| I | 70 | II | 75 | Longitude East | 80 | from Greenwich | 85 | V | 90 | VI |

to gain increased wealth and power. The imperial power, in this case Britain, is able to generate huge profits to develop its own nation, while the conquered territories experience a drain of wealth and resources. Britain and other European nations built empires in Africa and Asia during the Age of Imperialism. It is no coincidence that all of today's third-world countries were once part of a European country's empire.

At the same time, European governments justified their conquests.

They claimed they were advancing foreign colonies by conquering them, introducing them to Christianity, and making them "civilized" nations. The fact that foreigners did not eat, dress, or speak like the Europeans was referred to by Europeans as the "white man's burden."

The Revolt of 1857

Indians were unhappy with these developments. On May 10, 1857, Indian soldiers in the British army revolted in Meerut and marched

Lieutenant James Todd is seen on the back of an elephant in this nineteenth-century Indian painting, likely commissioned by the British. A principal leader in the British troop that secured India's Kingdom of Mysore in 1792, Todd was wounded in the attack. This painting is now housed in the Victoria and Albert Museum in London, England.

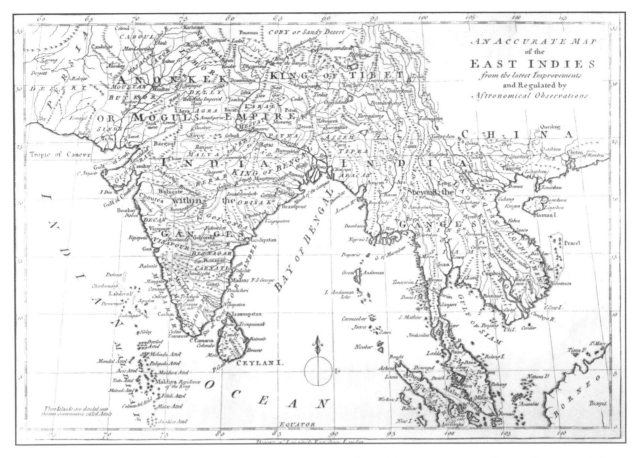

This map of the East Indies, dated 1780, shows India and neighboring countries during the time of the British Raj. The map's origin is unknown, but the land east of India known as Burma (present-day Myanmar) is labeled as "India beyond the Ganges."

60 miles (97 km) to Delhi, to the Mughal emperor.

At this time the emperor, Bahadur Shah II, was only a figurehead without power, but with this uprising, many Indians hoped to remove the British and re-establish Mughal rule.

There had before been several minor uprisings, but nothing of this size. Historians believe that this larger revolt was triggered by the conquest of Awadh in 1856, which was taken as an insult. Yet another insult to both Hindus and Muslims was the use of animal-greased bullets in the military, which was against Hinduism and Islam. (Both Hindus and Muslims do not eat or touch pork, the fat with which the bullets were greased.)

Soon the uprising spread throughout India. All the princes who had lost their land and peasants, traders who were faced with heavy taxes, and former officials and governors of

This gouache painting, now housed in London's British Library, depicts two British officers in colonial India around 1820. General Ochterlony, leader of the British army under Lord Hastings, defeated the Nepalese, chiefly the Gurkhas, a tribe of the western Himalayas, in the Anglo-Gurkha War (1814–1816), also known as the Nepalese War of 1814.

the Mughal government joined together. For a while it seemed as if the rebels might win. But the British had military superiority. They were able to suppress the uprising by 1859, massacring thousands. Many brave Indians, including Tantya Tope and the princess of Jhansi, Laxmibai, lost their lives in battle.

The British Government

The formal end of Mughal rule came in 1858, with Bahadur Shah exiled to Burma. It also marked the end of company rule. The British government immediately took over, later naming Queen Victoria the empress of India.

This change of rule did nothing to end the Indians' economic suffering. The British government continued its exploitation policies. A viceroy was appointed over the governor-general, and each province had local British officials of the Indian Civil Service. The government did end annexation, but that had little meaning, since all the 562 so-called independent princely states were now just run by powerless officials.

The British did, however, establish schools and ban some inhumane aspects of Hindu culture such as *sati* (the forced suicide of widows), child marriage, and infanticide.

6 THE FREEDOM STRUGGLE

British rule itself gave birth to the same means that ended its power. As British education spread among Indians, a new class of Western-educated professionals and merchants emerged. Lawyers, accountants, and bureaucrats, who studied Western philosophy and politics, now recognized the basic double standards of British leadership. While the British talked about democracy, freedom, and rights, they were oppressing the Indian people.

The Indian National Congress and the Muslim League

In 1885, a group of Indians from Bombay (Mumbai) and Calcutta, who had studied in England, met in Bombay and formed the Indian National Congress. Members included Surendranath Banerjea, Dadabhai Naoroji, Badruddin Tyabji, and M. G. Ranade. The goal of this organization was to lobby and petition the British to improve their government.

The congress wanted Indians to be included in the viceroy's council and provincial governments. It wanted more Indian representation in the bureaucracy, and it wanted the British to stop the "drain of wealth" from India. Ultimately, it wanted Britain to grant India the freedom to govern itself. It hoped

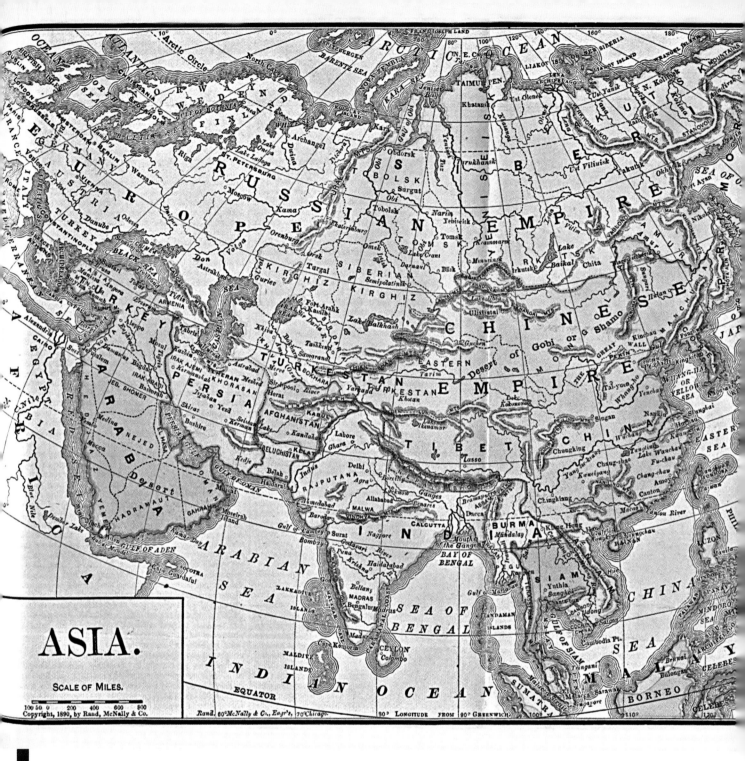

ASIA.

SCALE OF MILES.

100 50 0   200   400   600   800

Copyright, 1890, by Rand, McNally & Co.

Rand. 60°McNally & Co., Engr's, 70°Chicago.   80° LONGITUDE   FROM   90° GREENWICH. 100°

This historic map of Asia, first published in an Americanized version of *Encyclopedia Britannica*, shows how India appeared around 1892. It was during this period that the British had succeeded in annexing the majority of Indian states after the Indian Rebellion of 1857–1858, finally abolishing the East India Company. India then became a British colony ruled entirely by Queen Victoria and the British Crown.

to achieve these goals peacefully, through public speaking, petitions, and other negotiations.

It soon became clear that the British would not respond to peaceful petitions. In fact, the British partitioned the province of Bengal into east and west sections, further angering Hindus. Some leaders, like Bal Gangadhar Tilak, started organizing demonstrations, strikes, boycotts, and bonfires of British goods. The moderate congress soon became militant.

When congress formed, most Muslims were too afraid to join the organization. Having been severely suppressed after the revolt of 1857, Muslims fell behind in education, and fewer and fewer served the government. Many Muslims believed that their interests were different from those of the congress. They feared that if they joined it, they would lose the few opportunities they had.

After a while, some Muslim princes and businessmen decided to form their own party called the All India Muslim League. They were concerned that if the congress

succeeded in persuading the government to establish elected councils, Muslims, who were a minority, would have little say in them. They were joined by graduates of the Muhammadan Anglo-Oriental College in Aligarh, which was founded by Sir Sayyad Ahmad Khan to increase Muslim education.

In response to the congress's demands and increasing protests throughout India, the British enacted the Indian Councils Act in 1909. This act allowed Indians to contest elections. For the league, a percentage of seats were reserved for Muslims, guaranteeing them representation by a minimum number in the elected bodies.

Mahatma Gandhi

At the turn of the century, a new leader named Mohandas Karamchand Gandhi, also known as Mahatma (Great Soul), emerged in India. A lawyer from Gujarat, Gandhi returned from South Africa to take up a role in the freedom struggle. Soon he became the undisputed leader of the congress, with followers like Jawaharlal Nehru, and was successful in transforming the congress from an elite group to a mass organization.

Gandhi realized that it was important that Hindus and Muslims work together for independence.

Mohandas Gandhi (1869–1948), known as Mahatma, or the Great Soul, began his campaigns of civil disobedience in India in 1919. One of his greatest achievements was his ability to ease the killings caused by racial unrest between Hindus and Muslims in the 1940s. A Hindu extremist assassinated Gandhi because of his political opinions.

Amritsar, Punjab. Now known as the Jallianwala Bagh Massacre, the killings added to the Indians' outrage.

Gandhi persuaded the congress to support the Khilafat Movement. Soon it became the nationwide Non-Cooperation Movement using Gandhi's *satyagraha* (truthful struggle), based on nonviolence, which included non-cooperation, fasts, and strikes. Many congress and Muslim League workers were imprisoned for their actions.

The British did enact some more "reforms" in 1919, allowing more Indians to participate in government. They also promised that they would eventually let India become independent. The reforms, however, were far below the Indians' expectations. They had hoped for full control of some provinces and a greater say in the viceroy's council, so they continued to agitate.

Divided by electoral politics, the Muslim League split from the

With his influence, the congress and the Muslim League signed the Lucknow Pact in 1916.

At the time, many Muslims were worried that after World War I (1914–1918), the Ottoman caliphate would be ended by the victorious British. They launched an agitation called the Khilafat (Caliphate) Movement in 1919. The same year, the British massacred 397 people and wounded 1,137 others who had gathered to celebrate a spring festival in

The Indian Independence Act of 1947 *(right)*, drawn up after the British had decided to "quit" India, also separated Hindu India and the new Muslim nation of Pakistan. Upon India's independence, the nation's first prime minister, Jawaharlal Nehru, said in his speech to the Indian people, "[Our endeavor shall be] to bring freedom and opportunity to the common man; to end poverty and ignorance and disease; to build up a prosperous, democratic and progressive nation, and to create social, economic and political institutions which will ensure justice and fullness of life to every man and woman."

Section.
9.   Orders for bringing this Act into force.
10. Secretary of State's services, etc.
11. Indian armed forces.
12. British forces in India.
13. Naval forces.
14. Provisions as to the Secretary of State and the Auditor of Indian Home Accounts.
15. Legal proceedings by and against the Secretary of State.
16. Aden.
17. Divorce jurisdiction.
18. Provisions as to existing laws, etc.
19. Interpretation, etc.
20. Short title.
     SCHEDULES :
         First Schedule.—Bengal Districts provisionally included in the new Province of East Bengal.
         Second Schedule.—Districts provisionally included in the new Province of West Punjab.
         Third Schedule.—Modifications of Army Act and Air Force Act in relation to British forces.

An Act to make provision for the setting up in India of two independent Dominions, to substitute other provisions for certain provisions of the Government of India Act, 1935, which apply outside those Dominions, and to provide for other matters consequential on or connected with the setting up of those Dominions.

[18th July 1947.]

BE it enacted by the King's most Excellent Majesty, by and with the advice and consent of the Lords Spiritual and Temporal, and Commons, in this present Parliament assembled, and by the authority of the same, as follows :—

1.—(1) As from the fifteenth day of August, nineteen hundred and forty-scven, two independent Dominions shall be set up in India, to be known respectively as India and Pakistan. *The new Dominions.*

(2) The said Dominions are hereafter in this Act referred to as "the new Dominions", and the said fifteenth day of August is hereafter in this Act referred to as "the appointed day".

2.—(1) Subject to the provisions of subsections (3) and (4) of this section, the territories of India shall be the territories under the sovereignty of His Majesty which, immediately before the appointed day, were included in British India except the territories which, under subsection (2) of this section, are to be the territories of Pakistan. *Territories of the new Dominions.*

(2) Subject to the provisions of subsections (3) and (4) of this section, the territories of Pakistan shall be—

(a) the territories which, on the appointed day, are included in the Provinces of East Bengal and West Punjab, as constituted under the two following sections ;

The Hindus in this 1942 photograph were part of India's Quit India Movement (1942–1945), in which thousands marched, protested, and caused civil disturbances in an effort to push toward Indian independence. The Indian National Congress had passed the famous resolution in 1942 under the leadership of Gandhi, who stressed, "We shall either free India or die in the attempt."

break unfair British laws. He targeted a law that prevented Indians from making salt without paying tax. Gandhi led a march to Dandi on the Gujarat Coast and symbolically defied the government by picking a fistful of salt from the shore. The movement was a great success in mobilizing the Indian people, but the British became caught up in a bigger issue: World War II (1939–1945).

Independence

In both world wars, Britain used the British Indian army, deploying as many as 30 million soldiers, many of whom died. The viceroy even took taxes from Indians to give the government in London a "gift" of £10 million (at the time this figure was approximately $40 million).

In spite of all their contributions and suffering, the Indians were still treated badly. Gandhi launched another movement in 1942, called

congress. The league had argued that separate electorates (whereby Muslims voted for Muslim seats, and Hindus voted for Hindu) were the only way to ensure that Muslims were adequately represented. Now they argued that there should be a separate state within India for Muslims.

In 1935, Gandhi launched another struggle, the Civil Disobedience Movement. His aim was to peacefully

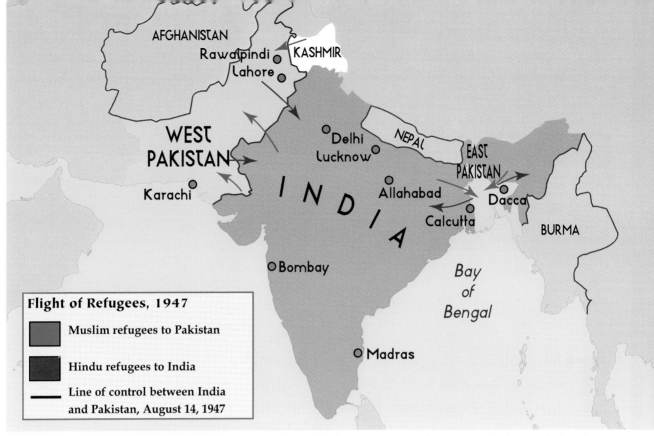

More than 7 million Muslims left India after Pakistan (both its eastern and western sides) was declared a separate nation in 1947, while a similar number of Hindus left the newly created Muslim country. The migration of both groups spurred massive violence and bloodshed that resulted in countless deaths. Some historians believe that more than 1 million people died in this transitional process, though an exact number is difficult to estimate. East Pakistan became the independent nation of Bangladesh in 1971.

"Quit India," asking the British to leave India immediately. The British promised that they would discuss this after the war.

After the war ended in 1945, the British held talks with the congress and the Muslim League. By now the Muslim League, led by Muhammad Ali Jinnah, wanted more than a separate state within India—it wanted a separate country. The British drew up a partition plan in which the Muslim-majority areas of Sindh, Baluchistan, Northwest Frontier Province, and half of Punjab in the west, as well as half of Bengal in the east, would be given to this new country, to be called Pakistan. The 562 "independent" princely states were given a choice to join either India or Pakistan.

The congress was against this, arguing that India was a nation of all religions. For two years, it tried to negotiate a compromise. But riots between Hindus and Muslims became more frequent. The British, under Viceroy Mountbatten, were desperate to "quit" the mess they had created, and in 1947, they passed the India Independence Act, leaving their empire of 200 years in just a couple of months. India and Pakistan then became independent on the night of August 14–15, 1947.

7 INDIA AFTER INDEPENDENCE

The moment of greatest joy—independence—was also one of the most painful for India. Power had passed smoothly in India to the congress, led by Jawaharlal Nehru, and in Pakistan to the Muslim League, led by Muhammad Ali Jinnah, but the separation was not smooth. Many Hindus lived in what is now Pakistan, and many Muslims still lived in India. Hindus and Muslims tried to cross the borders, which led to the "swapping" of populations. But emotions and anger ran high, leading to riots and massacres. Historians estimate that 1 million people lost their lives during Partition.

The Nehruvian Era (1947–1962)

Prime Minister Nehru had a tough task ahead of him. He had lost his mentor, Mahatma Gandhi, who was gunned down in 1948 by

This present-day map of India also shows Pakistan, Bangladesh (formerly East Pakistan and made independent in 1971), and the disputed territory of Jammu and Kashmir. India faces a difficult future of quelling religious violence between Hindus and Muslims as well as struggling to maintain a peaceful relationship with Pakistan, a marriage between two nuclear-capable nations that has remained strained into the new century.

PAKISTAN

Hyderabad
Karachi
Indus

ARABIAN
SEA

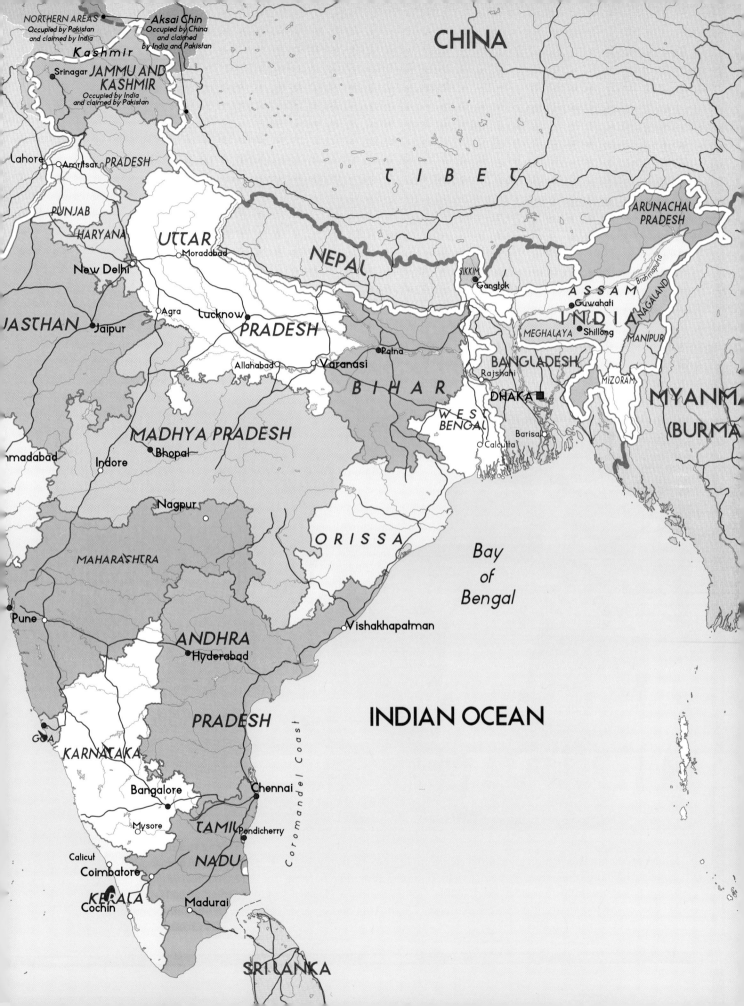

a Hindu militant who blamed Gandhi for Partition.

There was also the question of the princely states. Most of them readily joined India, but three, Hyderabad, Jammu and Kashmir, and Junagadh, threatened to join Pakistan. The army was sent in, forcing Hyderabad and Junagadh to join India. In Jammu and Kashmir, 90 percent of the people were Muslims, but the state was ruled by a Hindu king, Hari Singh, who was undecided. In 1948, when Pakistan sent in its army, Singh took India's help and Jammu and Kashmir joined India, but Pakistan held on to some parts. India and Pakistan have been fighting over Jammu and Kashmir ever since.

In the meantime, Indians wrote their own constitution, forming a semifederal parliamentary republic. The constitution specifies that India is a secular democratic nation, meaning state and religion are separate and all religions have equal rights. It

Indian prime minister Pandit Jawaharlal Nehru (right) reviews troops of the Rajputana Rifles at Independence Day flag-hoisting ceremonies in August 1948, one year after India became free of British rule. Walking behind Nehru is Defense Minister Baldev Singh (white coat and turban). General Sir Roy Bucher, British commander-in-chief of the Indian army, walks beside Baldev Singh. This photograph was taken in Bombay (Mumbai).

was adopted on January 26, 1950. This date is now celebrated as Republic Day.

Centuries of British rule had left India poor and undeveloped. Nehru was determined to make India an industrial power. Using economic planning, the government built large electric dams, steel mills, and coal mines.

Nehru was also concerned by the Cold War between the United States and the Union of Soviet Socialist Republics (U.S.S.R.). Wanting to remain neutral, India, along with other newly independent nations, formed the Non-Aligned Movement. India also fought a war with China in 1962 over border disputes. China claimed that the northernmost part of Kashmir, Aksai Chin, was really part of its Xinkiang province. India lost the war, but China withdrew from all the territory it won, except Aksai Chin.

Indira Takes Over

When Nehru died in 1964, Lal Bahadur Shastri took over as leader of the congress and won the 1965 war against Pakistan. Shastri died in 1966, and Nehru's daughter, Indira Gandhi (who was married to Feroze Gandhi, no relation to Mahatma Gandhi), became prime minister.

Initially she was a popular leader, continuing her father's legacy. In 1971, when Pakistanis (Bengalis) broke away from East Pakistan, she helped them form their own nation, Bangladesh.

Over time, she grew autocratic, which means she ruled as an absolute dictator. She implemented unjust policies, such as forced sterilization to help control overpopulation. Soon there were nationwide protests against her leadership. Panicked, Indira Gandhi enforced a national emergency in June 1975. All civil and political rights of citizens were suspended, but problems continued.

Indira Gandhi (1917–1984) was one of India's most controversial leaders. She acted as the country's prime minister from 1966 to 1977 and from 1980 to 1984. Though most Indians felt her leadership became too authoritative, she was a passionate administrator.

In 1977, she called elections, hoping to placate the people. Instead, a coalition led by the Janata Party came to power, but their coalition crumbled. Elections were held in 1979, and Indira Gandhi won.

In the 1980s, the Sikhs in Punjab began agitating for a separate state, Khalistan. They felt the Indian government discriminated against them, not providing good jobs or industries in Punjab. The Khalistan extremists took over the holiest Sikh shrine, the Golden Temple in Amritsar, in 1984. Indira sent in the army, leading to a four-day battle in which hundreds of Sikhs died. The Khalistanis took revenge by assassinating her on October 31, 1984. Hindus retaliated by killing thousands of Sikhs in Delhi.

Increasing Turmoil

After Indira was killed, her elder son, Rajiv, took over. Under Rajiv, the army fought bloody battles with the Sikhs, as well as militants in Jammu and Kashmir who were fighting for independence. He even sent the army to Sri Lanka, where Tamils were fighting a separatist war of their own. Other countries started to see India as a bully, so Rajiv helped establish the South Asian Association for Regional Cooperation to improve ties with India's neighbors. In 1989, Rajiv lost general elections over corruption allegations. He was assassinated by a Sri Lankan suicide bomber in 1991.

India's new prime minister, V. P. Singh, was respected for his honesty but was the head of another fragile coalition. One of his partners, the Indian People's Party (BJP), withdrew support in 1990 when Singh refused to let them march to Ayodhya. It was there that the BJP wanted to take over the Babri Mosque, which they claimed was once a temple marking the birthplace of Lord Ram and had been demolished by the Mughals. The BJP openly says it doesn't believe in secularism; according to the party secularism means discrimination against Hindus. It argues that Indians who are not Hindu are foreigners and have no business living in India.

Unfortunately, over time the BJP's ideology gained popularity among some Indians. This was partly due to educational backwardness, lack of job opportunities, and discontent among India's middle classes. The BJP provided these groups with scapegoats— mostly minorities and especially Muslims—on whom to blame their frustrations.

In 1992, the BJP succeeded in leading another march to Ayodhya, and this time it demolished the

This photograph shows an activist of India's People's Democratic Party (PDP) as he cheers while Mehbooba Mufti *(right)*, vice president of the PDP, is greeted by supporters at her residence on the outskirts of Srinagar on October 28, 2002. Mehbooba Mufti has pushed for improved human rights in India. Mufti's father and PDP chief, Mufti Mohammad Sayeed, was named the chief minister of the (disputed) Indian state of Jammu and Kashmir.

mosque even as the government watched. This led to some of the worst Hindu-Muslim riots since Partition. Thousands died.

The BJP came to power for a few months in 1998, until the party lost the majority support of parliament in early 1999. While in power, Prime Minster Atal Behari Vajpayee ordered testing of nuclear bombs. The world was shocked and worried by the consequences, given India's hostility with Pakistan, which responded with tests of its own.

After another election in 1999, the BJP was back in power, with Vajpayee at the helm again. Most Hindus do not support the BJP, but it is able to stay in power since no other political party is strong enough to win elections.

The Indian government has had a poor track record of dealing with important issues like underdevelopment, poverty, and hunger. Most of the people are growing poorer, but a tiny fraction living in cities live lavish lifestyles copied from the West. The government does not uphold the value of secularism and actually encourages discord. There are increasing incidents of religious violence and chances of war with Pakistan. In 1999, several Australian missionaries were burned alive. In March 2002, in the state of Gujarat, thousands (mostly Muslims) died in religious violence. Independent investigations showed that the police and the government did nothing to stop the killers and may have even helped them. Given such scenarios, many Indians are worried about the future. They want India to remain a secular democracy in which all religions and all people can flourish.

TIMELINE

2000 BC The civilizations of Harappa and Mohenjo-Daro flourish.

1500 BC The Aryans invade India, defeating the Harappans.

563 BC Siddhartha Gautama is born.

530 BC The Persians conquer Gandhara under Cyrus the Great.

528 BC Gautama reaches enlightenment and is known as Buddha.

327 BC Alexander the Great leads the Greeks into India.

269 BC Ashoka takes power and becomes a Buddhist.

AD 100 The Kushanas gain control of northern India.

700–1300 The period marking the rise of the Rajput kings.

1000–1026 Mahmud of Ghazni repeatedly attacks Punjab.

1192 The beginning of the Muslim Delhi sultanate.

1398 Timur sacks Delhi. Hindu kingdoms dominate southern India.

1498 Vasco da Gama reaches India.

1526 Babur takes Delhi and Agra, beginning the Mughal Empire.

1556–1605 Akbar unites India and allows freedom of religion.

1600 Queen Elizabeth I grants trading rights to the British.

1640 The British build a trading capital at Madras.

1707 The Mughal Empire begins to decline.

1765 Mughal leaders grant the British the right to Bengali revenues.

1799 Tipu Sultan, the "Tiger of Mysore," falls to the British.

1849 After two Sikh conflicts, the British take Punjab.

1857 Indian foot soldiers in the British army declare support for the Mughals.

1885 Formation of the Indian National Congress (INC).

1906 Formation of the All India Muslim League.

1914 World War I begins.

1915 Mahatma Gandhi requests that the INC include all castes.

1920s–1947 Tension increases between the INC and the Muslim League.

1947 India wins independence from Britain.

1948 Gandhi is assassinated by a Hindu extremist.

1964 Indira Gandhi is voted into office.

1971 Civil war in East Pakistan. East Pakistan becomes Bangladesh.

1974 India detonates its first nuclear device.

1996 Shri Atal Behari Vajpayee is voted into office.

1997 Kocheril Raman Narayanan is elected president.

1998 India tests its nuclear missiles.

1999 The Indian People's Party (BJP) gains control.

2000 Relations between India and Pakistan improve when Vajpayee travels to meet Sharif.

2001 India imposes sanctions on Pakistan. Violence in Jammu and Kashmir continues.

2002 A. P. J. Abdul Kalam is sworn in as India's eleventh president. Violence against Muslims in India erupts, resulting in the deaths of hundreds.

2003 Both President Kalam and Prime Minister Vajpayee voice opposition of the United States–led incursion into Iraq.

GLOSSARY

Brahman The absolute reality; the eternal, supreme, or ultimate principle; a state of pure transcendence; a supreme being who is the cause of the universe.

Brahmin From the Sanskrit *brahmana*, one of four major caste groups (varna) or social classes. Brahmins are the highest caste group, traditionally made up of priests, philosophers, scholars, and religious leaders.

British Raj The period of direct rule of India by the British government (1858–1947), marking the end of the Mughal Empire and the beginning of the East India Company rule.

caste system A system originally developed in the Ganges valley around 500 BC that grouped people in strict socioeconomic divisions.

Cold War A condition of rivalry and mistrust between the United States and the Soviet Union in the mid- to late twentieth century.

Devnagari "The script of the city of the gods"; script used to write Sanskrit, Hindi, and Marathi.

dharma In Hinduism and Buddhism, moral duty, or moral code of proper conduct.

guru In the Sikh faith, one of ten spiritual leaders, the first of whom was Nanak Dev, the last being Gobind Singh; in Hinduism, a religious teacher or guide.

karma Literally means action; spiritual merit or demerit that a being acquired in a previous incarnation and is acquiring in present existence.

martial law Laws applied by military force during an occupation of any certain territory.

monotheism The belief in one god.

Non-Aligned Movement Established in September 1961 with the aim of promoting the concept of political and military nonalignment apart from the traditional east and west blocs. India was among the original member nations.

nonalignment The ideological basis of Indian foreign policy, first articulated by Jawaharlal Nehru; refusal to align India with any alliance; peaceful settlement of international disputes.

Partition A term used for the division of Asian land into India and Pakistan in 1947.

secular Nonreligious.

satyagraha Method employed by Mahatma Gandhi and his followers to secure sociopolitical reform by nonviolent, passive resistance and non-cooperation; the individual following the method is called a *satyagrahi*.

swadeshi "Of my country"; a part of the freedom struggle that emphasized boycott of British goods and use of only Indian-made items.

varna "Color"; one of the four large caste groups—Brahmin, Kshatriya, Vaishya, and Sudra—from which subcastes are derived.

zamindar Landlord; a person who owned the land, but who allowed or forced peasants to farm on it in return for a share of the produce.

FOR MORE INFORMATION

American Institute of Indian Studies
1130 East Fifty-ninth Street
Chicago, IL 60637
(773) 702-8638
Web site: http://www.indiastudies.org

Embassy of India
2107 Massachusetts Avenue
Washington, DC 20008
(202) 939 7000
Web site:
http://www.indianembassy.org

Web sites

Due to the changing nature of Internet links, the Rosen Publishing Group, Inc., has developed an online list of Web sites related to the subject of this book. This site is updated regularly. Please use this link to access the list:

http://www.rosenlinks.com/liha/indi

FOR FURTHER READING

Basham, A. L., ed. *Cultural History of India*. London: Oxford University Press, 1998.

Draper, Alison Stark. *India: A Primary Source Cultural Guide*. New York: The Rosen Publishing Group, Inc., 2003.

Keay, John. *India: A History*. Boston: Atlantic Monthly Press, 2001.

Malaspina, Ann. *Mahatma Gandi and India's Independence in World History* (In World History). Berkeley Heights, NJ: Enslow Publishers, 2000.

Metcalf, Barbara D. *A Concise History of India*. Boston: Cambridge University Press, 2001.

Wagner, Heather Lehr. *India and Pakistan* (People at Odds). Broomall, PA: Chelsea House Publishers, 2002.

BIBLIOGRAPHY

Chandler, Satiate. *Medieval India*. New Delhi: National Council of Educational Training and Research, 1999.

"India." *Encyclopedia Britannica*. Retrieved September 15, 2002 (http://www.britannica.com/eb/article?eu=121168).

"India." Library of Congress Country Studies, 1995. Retrieved September 25, 2002 (http://lcweb2.loc.gov/frd/cs/intoc.html).

Jalal, Ayesha, and Sugata Bose, ed. "Exploding Communalism: The Politics of Muslim Identity in South Asia." *Nationalism, Democracy and Development*. New Delhi: Oxford University Press, 1997.

Kay, John. *India: A History*. New York: Grove Press, 2000.

Searcher, Summit. *Modern India 1885–1974*. New Delhi: Macmillan India, 1986.

Trapper, Remittal. *A History of India*, Vol. 1. New Delhi: Penguin, 1991.

INDEX

A

Afghanistan, 20, 21, 28, 31, 32, 33, 37
Aibak, Qutubuddin, 28
Akbar, Jalaluddin, 32–34
Alexander the Great, 17
Arabs/Arabia, 21, 23, 26, 28
art/literature, 15, 21, 33, 34
Aryans, 12, 13–16
Ashoka, 17–20
Aurangzeb, 35–37, 40

B

Babur, Zahiruddin, 31–32
Bahadur Shah II, 45, 46
Bangladesh, 5, 20, 57
Buddha (Gautama Buddha), 16, 21
Buddhism, 7, 16, 20, 23

C

caste system (varnas), 14–16, 23, 24, 26, 27
Chandragupta Maurya, 17
China, 5, 16, 21, 42, 57
Cholas, 29–30
Christianity, 7, 44
Clive, Robert, 40
constitution, 56–57

D

Delhi sultanate, 29, 31
Dravidians, 23

E

East India Trading Company, 40–42, 46
education, 21, 46, 47, 49, 58
Europeans, 37, 38, 44

F

feudalism, 24, 29

G

Gandhi, Indira, 57–58
Gandhi, Mahatma, 49–50, 52–53, 54–56, 57
Gandhi, Rajiv, 58
Genghis Khan, 31
gods, 14, 15, 23

Great Britain

Great Britain, 7, 38, 40–46, 47–49, 50, 52–53, 57
Guptas, 21–22

H

Harappan Civilization, 8–12, 13, 23
Hinduism/Hindus, 7, 14, 21, 23, 29, 37, 45, 49–50, 52, 56
  and caste system, 27
  fighting with Muslims, 53, 54, 59
  and Indian People's Party, 58–59
  literature, 14
  negative aspects of, 34, 46
  and Sikhism, 35

I

imperialism, 42–44
independence, 53, 54, 57
India, facts about, 5–7
Indian National Congress, 47–49, 50, 53, 54, 57
Indian People's Party (BJP), 58–59
Islam/Muslims, 7, 26–28, 29, 34, 37, 45, 52
  fighting with Hindus, 53, 54, 58–59
  and formation of Pakistan, 53, 54, 56
  and Muslim League, 49–50
  and Sikhism, 35

J

Jahangir, 34, 35
Jainism, 7, 23
Jallianwala Bagh Massacre, 50
Jinnah, Muhammad Ali, 53, 54

K

Khilafat Movement, 50
kingdoms, 22–23, 24–26, 28–30
Kushanas, 21

M

Mamluks, 28
Marathas, 37, 41
Mauryan Empire, 17–21, 22
Mongols, 31
Mughals, 31–37, 38, 40, 45–46, 58
Muhammad, 26, 27–28
Muhammad of Ghor, 28
Muslim League, 49, 50–52, 53, 54

N

Nehru, Jawaharlal, 49, 54, 57

P

Pakistan, 5, 10, 53, 54, 56, 57, 59
Partition, 53, 54, 56, 59
Prakrit, 13, 20

R

Rajputs, 26, 28, 29, 32, 34, 41
revolt of 1857, 44–46, 49

S

Sanskrit, 7, 13, 23
science/math, 7, 21, 33
Shah Jahan, 34–35
Sher Shah Suri, 32, 33
Sikhism/Sikhs, 7, 35, 37, 41, 58
Singh, V. P., 59

T

Timur, 31
trade, 11, 17, 20, 21, 23, 26, 29, 33–34, 38, 40–41, 42, 45
Turks, 28, 29, 30, 31

V

Vajpayee, Atal Behari, 59

W

World War II, 52, 53

About the Author

Aisha Khan is a journalist from India now living in New York. She has always had a fascination with central and south Asia.

Photo Credits

Cover (map), pp. 1 (foreground), 4–5, 54–55 © Geoatlas; cover (background), pp. 1 (background), 6–7, 36, 43, 48–49 courtesy of the General Libraries, the University of Texas at Austin; cover (top left), cover (bottom right), pp. 14, 35 © The Art Archive/British Library; cover (bottom left), p. 59 © AP/Wide World Photos; pp. 8–9, 18–19, 20–21, 22, 27, 53 maps designed by Tahara Hasan; pp. 9 (inset), 12 © The Art Archive/National Museum Karachi/Dagli Orti; p. 10 © Diego Lezama Orezzoli/Corbis; pp. 11, 23 © Charles and Josette Lenars/Corbis; p. 15 © Lindsay Hebberd/Corbis; pp. 16, 26, 34 © AKG London/Jean-Louis Nou; pp. 17, 44 © The Art Archive/Victoria and Albert Museum London/Sally Chappell; pp. 24–25 © The Art Archive/Maritiem Museum Prins Hendrik Rotterdam/Dagli Orti; p. 28 © Paul Almasy/Corbis; p. 32 © Angelo Hornak/Corbis; p. 33 © Philadelphia Museum of Art/Corbis; pp. 38–39, 45 © Mary Evans Picture Library; p. 40 © The Art Archive/India Office Library; p. 41 © The Art Archive/Arquivo Nacional da Torre do Tombo Lisbon/ Dagli Orti; p. 46 © AKG London/British Library; pp. 50, 56, 57 © Bettmann/Corbis; p. 51 © Dinodia; p. 52 © AKG/London.

Designer: Tahara Hasan; **Editor:** Joann Jovinelly; **Photo Researcher:** Elizabeth Loving